VANISHED

TRUE TALES OF MYSTERIOUS DISAPPEARANCES

ELIZABETH MACLEOD

annick
press
toronto•berkeley

Edited by Chandra Wohleber
Designed by Sheryl Shapiro

Third printing, August 2021

Annick Press Ltd.

We acknowledge the support of the Canada Council for the Arts, the Ontario Arts Council, and the participation of the Government of Canada/la participation du gouvernement du Canada for our publishing activities.

Canada

ONTARIO ARTS COUNCIL
CONSEIL DES ARTS DE L'ONTARIO
an Ontario government agency
un organisme du gouvernement de l'Ontario

Cataloging in Publication

MacLeod, Elizabeth, author
    Vanished : true tales of mysterious disappearances / Elizabeth MacLeod.

Includes bibliographical references and index.
Issued in print and electronic formats.
ISBN 978-1-55451-818-0 (bound).–ISBN 978-1-55451-817-3 (paperback).–
ISBN 978-1-55451-819-7 (epub).–ISBN 978-1-55451-820-3 (pdf)

    1. Disappearances (Parapsychology)–Juvenile literature. 2. Missing persons–Juvenile literature. 3. Curiosities and wonders–Juvenile literature. I. Title.

BF1389.D57M3 2016   j001.94   C2015-905351-X
                                            C2015-905352-8

Published in the U.S.A. by Annick Press (U.S.) Ltd.
Distributed in Canada by University of Toronto Press.
Distributed in the U.S.A. by Publishers Group West.

Printed in Canada.

Visit us at: www.annickpress.com

Also available in e-book format. Please visit www.annickpress.com/ebooks.html for more details.

CONTENTS

With much love and admiration for Cathi,
eine ausgezeichtnete Freundin and someone
who I hope never vanishes from my life!

WITHOUT A TRACE ...

All over the world and all through history, people—individuals and entire groups—large amounts of money, famous artworks, and even whole ships have vanished. Some leave tantalizing clues, while others leave not a trace. The tales behind some of the world's most mystifying disappearances have captivated historians and other experts for centuries.

Why did the person or object disappear? *What* clues exist about where it is? *Who* knows or knew about the case? *How* can new technologies and techniques help to finally solve the mystery?

Disappearances happen for many reasons. In times of war, rebellion, and political or religious uprisings, people hide money and valuable objects so well, they're never found again. Of course someone once knew where the treasure was hidden, but the story is lost if that person dies without revealing the secret.

People may disappear because someone wants them out of the way in a competition for the throne or another position of power. Brutal political regimes or fanatical groups have "disappeared" whole communities that disagree with them. Or people vanish because they take on a new identity to avoid being found by the police or their families. Natural disasters and accidents can also make things disappear, especially in remote places like barely inhabited islands or the middle of the ocean.

Today, electronic banking records, security cameras, cell phone triangulation, DNA matching, robotics, sonar equipment, and Internet activity make it much easier to locate people and objects. Even so, some intriguing cases of disappearances remain unsolved. As technology continues to develop, perhaps experts will be able to track down more evidence of the location of vanished objects and may finally discover what happened to people long gone. That hope turns many stories into legends shrouded in mystery.

Why do we keep searching? Maybe we just can't admit that something might be gone forever. Maybe it's like an especially challenging game we want to win. Or maybe we feel we'll understand an event or person or time period better if we can just uncover that secret.

In this book you'll meet mysteries that have not been solved. However, every day, scientists and historians are finding new ways to explore the past and make what is missing visible again. These technologies weren't available at the time of the events but might help solve the mysteries now, because perhaps what people love even more than a mystery is finally solving it—locating something or someone the world thought had disappeared … without a trace.

LOST COLONY

THE SETTLERS WHO DISAPPEARED

ROANOKE ISLAND, NORTH CAROLINA, 1590

Governor John White struggled through the tall grasses.
Did he have the wrong
place? No, he was sure the
colony had been right here
when he'd had to leave three
years ago. But he could find
no trace of the homes or other
buildings—or of the settlers.
Where the settlement had
stood, small trees now stretched up toward the sun and thick
grasses covered the area.

   "Spread out and search for any sign of them," White com-
manded his men. "They must be here somewhere. More
than a hundred people cannot simply vanish. It staggers the
imagination."

   But as the moments ticked by and the crew examined the
area, it seemed Governor White was wrong. There was no sign
of the colonists, no matter how carefully they searched. White
called out the names of his daughter, his son-in-law, and his
granddaughter until he was hoarse, but there was no answer.
His voice echoed sadly around the site.

Governor John White and his men were relieved to at least find a trace of the settlers from the Lost Colony. But where had they gone?

"Sir, look," cried one of White's crew suddenly, pointing to a nearby tree trunk. The searchers rushed over and looked up. There, carved into the bark, were the letters CRO. On a post close by was the word CROATOAN. Finally, a sign that White had the right place.

"But what can be the meaning of this?" asked White perplexed. "Where are my family and all the other colonists? How can they have disappeared, every one of them?"

VOYAGE TO THE NEW WORLD

Three years ago, on May 8, 1587, Governor John White had set sail from England with 116 men, women, and children, including his daughter and son-in-law. White was filled with excitement and hope because it was his job to set up the first British colony in what is known today as North America.

European countries called this territory (as well as Central and South America) the New World, and they all wanted to stake a claim to it and set up colonies there. They believed more land meant more power. The fact that Native Americans were already living there didn't slow them down.

The famous British explorer Sir Walter Raleigh was behind the effort, as he had been for previous attempts to colonize the east coast of North America. But none had been successful, mostly because the earlier settlers and soldiers had made enemies of some of the Native people.

But this time, the colonists were determined to make the settlement work despite the dangers. They were proud to be representing such a

WALTER RALEIGH

In addition to being an explorer, Sir Walter Raleigh was a writer, soldier, politician, and spy. He was very important in England's colonization of North America.

THE AGE OF DISCOVERY

England's desire to establish a colony in what is now North America was part of the Age of Discovery. Beginning in the early 1400s, Europeans began to explore the rest of the world.

Spain focused on the Caribbean, Central America, and South America. Other countries, such as England, France, and Portugal, heard stories of treasures and riches in the New World (North, South, and Central America) and wanted their share. Later, explorers would discover such countries as Australia, in 1606, and New Zealand, in 1642.

The Age of Discovery led to a vast transfer of animals, cultures, and diseases between Europe and the New World. Europeans created maps of the areas they traveled, and distant civilizations came in contact with each other. The cultures had to change the way they thought about each other—and themselves.

well-known man as Raleigh in the New World. Little did they know that his fame and fortune may have already decided their fates.

White's pilot, Simon Fernandez, was Portuguese and had once been a pirate. However, just before he was to die for his crimes, an important British official had decided he should live. Soon after, Fernandez began navigating ships for England. One of the ships he navigated carried this group of colonists headed for Chesapeake Bay on the northeast coast of the land now known as the United States. The soil in that area was said to be rich and fertile, and the bay provided a safe harbor.

But in July 1587, Fernandez dropped the settlers at the island of Roanoke instead of at Chesapeake Bay. The island got its name from the tribe of Native people living there—*roanoke* is an Algonquian word meaning "shell money." Fernandez explained that the voyage to the New World had taken too long (two and a half months) and that it was already too late in the year for him to carry them on to Chesapeake Bay. As the bay was actually only a few days' sail away, it's more likely Fernandez wanted to hurry off to join other pirates attacking Spanish ships.

A GRISLY DISCOVERY

Roanoke Island was not a location White would have chosen for the colony. An earlier English colony had failed there because the soldiers who settled on the land treated the Native people brutally and the Native people retaliated. Supply ships from England wouldn't have known about the last-minute change of location, and so wouldn't land there; no one would even know the settlers were on that island.

When White and his colonists arrived on Roanoke, among the first things they saw were bones—human bones. The buildings had been burned to the ground and the settlers never discovered exactly what had happened to the soldiers. It was unlikely the neighboring tribes would be helpful to another group of English settlers, which was why White had planned to establish his colony on the safer banks of Chesapeake Bay.

But White decided to make the best of the situation. With the help of Chief Manteo, head of a local tribe, White made contact with friendly Native people.

Historians have identified this as an illustration of Chief Manteo (front and back), with his hunting bow and arrows.

CHIEF MANTEO

Chief Manteo was a Croatan Native American who became friendly with the English. In 1584, he sailed with them to England, one of the first Native Americans to cross the Atlantic Ocean. Manteo returned to Roanoke Island in 1585 and helped the settlers survive the winter by teaching them what plants to eat and how to build warm homes. He sailed back to England in 1586, and in 1587 was on the ship that carried the settlers whose fate would become a mystery.

Manteo was christened on Roanoke Island—the first Native American to be baptized into the Church of England. Because he was a guide and translator for the English, some Native people felt he was a traitor. Like the settlers of the Lost Colony, the fate of this chief is unknown. The town of Manteo, near where experts believe the Lost Colony was founded, is named after him.

There was no time for the colonists to think about what had happened to the soldiers—they needed to get to work building their homes.

Soon after landing, White's daughter, Eleanor Dare, gave birth to a little girl, named Virginia Dare. She was the first person born to English parents in the New World. The colonists took this as a symbol of hope: perhaps their settlement would succeed after all.

DESPERATE TIMES

However, the colonists soon realized that they would run out of food. All they had to get them through the harsh winter was dried meat and fish, as well as the vegetables and grains they had brought with them—and it wasn't enough. They had arrived too late in the year to plant crops and harvest them before winter.

The settlers decided that White should head back to England for supplies, then return to Roanoke as quickly as he could. The governor didn't want to leave his family and the other colonists because he feared people back in England would think badly of him for abandoning them. But the settlers insisted that he go back to get help. So in August 1587, White set off across the ocean, promising to return with food and supplies as fast as possible. After all, his family and more than 100 other people were depending on him to return before winter set in.

Dried fish were an important food for people in the Roanoke Colony because the fish could be stored for a long time. The fish were dried in the open air using sun and wind.

Virginia Dare was the first child born to English parents and baptized (shown here) in North America. She was named after the Virginia Colony, the first English colony in the world.

VIRGINIA DARE

Like the fate of the rest of the Lost Colony, Virginia Dare's fate is unknown. But she has become an important figure in American mythology. To some, she symbolizes innocence; to others, new beginnings, adventure, and mystery. In the 1980s, one North Carolina group rallied people in their state to approve the Equal Rights Amendment and "Honor Virginia Dare."

Today, many locations are named after her, including Dare County in North Carolina and Virginia Dare Memorial Bridge, which extends over Croatan Sound to Roanoke Island. Dare was also shown on a commemorative half-dollar coin, making her the first child to appear on United States currency.

AN OCEAN AWAY

Just two weeks before White arrived home, England's Queen Elizabeth I issued an order preventing all ships from leaving England. England was at war with Spain and needed its ships to battle the Spanish Armada. Sir Walter Raleigh felt sorry for the abandoned settlers back in Roanoke and tried to provide White with ships to sail across the Atlantic and save the colonists, but the queen refused to allow the rescue attempt. White was trapped in England.

The governor refused to give up. After all, the settlers were relying on him. In early 1588, he found two small ships that had been judged unsuitable for fighting and so could be spared to journey to Roanoke. But soon after White set out, French pirates attacked his ships and stole everything on board. White and his crew barely escaped back to England with their lives.

François Lolonois was one of the best-known French pirates. He was famous for his ferocity and cruelty.

Between 1585 and 1604, England and Spain were often at war. In 1588, a fleet of 130 Spanish ships, called the Armada, set sail for England.

The queen finally allowed Raleigh to send White to Roanoke two years later, in March 1590. The weather was terrible during the voyage, and White's two ships were again attacked by pirates. White didn't reach Roanoke Island until August 18, 1590, what would have been little Virginia Dare's third birthday. The conditions and currents offshore were so rough that seven members of the crew drowned trying to land the ships at Roanoke. And then, when he finally reached the shore, what White found there made his blood run cold.

LOST JUNGLE CITY

Hidden deep in a vast rain forest in the Central American country of Honduras lies an ancient city. Until 2015, the city was lost in the thick jungle, despite almost a century of expeditions to locate it.

The explorers were searching for a legendary city known as the "White City" or the "City of the Monkey God." It is believed to have been home to a civilization that vanished without a trace about 1,000 years ago.

Using a plane and a remote-sensing technique known as Lidar (see page 31), archaeologists discovered mounds and an earthen pyramid. They also found stone sculptures, including thrones likely used by the community's leaders, and giant carved bowls. The scientists believe the artifacts have not been touched for several centuries.

Elizabeth I was queen of England from 1558 to 1603. Her defeat of the Spanish Armada (see page 13) was one of the greatest battle victories in England's history.

GONE TO CROATOAN

There was not a trace of any of the colonists. The fort they'd built three years ago was lying in pieces and almost everything else—weapons, tools, and other belongings—had vanished. But White saw no sign of battle—or of graves.

White had taken precautions before he'd left the settlers three years earlier. Together, they'd arranged what the colonists should do so White could find them if they had to leave the island. They were to carve on a tree the name of the place they were going. If they were being forced to leave against their will, they agreed to carve a Maltese cross, an eight-pointed symbol, over the name of the new location.

Now, White and his men saw the name CROATOAN carved on the post. They knew that was the name of a nearby island, as well as the name of a tribe of Native people in the area who had been friendly to the English. Quickly scanning the post for the Maltese cross, White saw no sign of it. He breathed a little easier.

White could tell that the colonists' houses and palisades (fences made of pointed pieces of wood or iron) had been taken apart, not destroyed in panic or conflict. From this, he deduced that the settlers hadn't needed to leave the site quickly. But still, *Where were they?*

The Maltese cross is an eight-pointed cross. It gets its name from a group of knights who were based on the island of Malta in the Mediterranean Sea.

A palisade, or fence made of tree trunks, surrounds this Native village located near the Roanoke Colony. That settlement was enclosed by a similar barricade.

SEARCHING IN VAIN

White was determined to find the colonists. He worried that maybe something so bad had happened, they hadn't had time to carve the Maltese cross. He decided to sail the 72 kilometers (45 miles) to Croatoan immediately to see what he could discover.

But before White could go any-where, a vicious hurricane blew up. His ship was damaged and car-ried out to sea on the high winds and rolling waves. Despite White's desperate pleas, the captain refused to spend more time looking for the colonists. The voyage had already been so bad that the ship had lost three anchors. It couldn't afford to lose another, so the captain decided there would be no more stops.

White was forced to return to England without conducting any fur-ther searches. He must have watched with despair as the ship headed out into the Atlantic Ocean and the New World disappeared below the horizon.

A few months later, White returned to the area, but again, bad weather forced him to turn back before he could search for the Lost Colony. Heartbroken, White couldn't raise enough money to journey to the New World again. He never received any more information about his daughter, son-in-law, or grand-daughter. White died a disappointed man in about 1593, but he never gave up hope that his daughter and her family were living safely with the Croatoans.

The tallest of the famous stone statues on Easter Island is as tall as a three-story building.

EASTER ISLAND

Famous for its almost 900 huge statues, called *moai,* Easter Island was also home to a now-lost civilization. Polynesian people settled there more than 1,000 years ago. They created a thriving, advanced civilization, capable of incredible navigation between the far-flung islands in the area, as well as remarkable construction and artwork.

In the early 1600s, the population of Easter Island was about 15,000, but a century later, it had dropped to as few as 2,000. The people had used up all of the island's trees and other natural resources. Diseases introduced by European sailors and traders also had a fatal effect on the Rapa Nui, the people of Easter Island, and by 1877, only 111 people lived there. More than half of the almost 6,000 people living on the island today are related to the Rapa Nui, but, sadly, much of the island's culture and knowledge has been lost.

EPIDEMICS, KIDNAPPINGS, AND SHIPWRECKS

In the summer of 1588, a scouting party from a Spanish expedition visited Roanoke and found that the settlement had already been abandoned. In 1607, the English built a settlement in Jamestown, Virginia, that was successful and became the first permanent English settlement in North America. It wasn't until then, 20 years after the colonists had last been seen, that more search parties finally went looking for them. Settlers from Jamestown found only hints and rumors from Native people about survivors of the Lost Colony.

What could have happened to the colonists? It's unlikely that they starved to death because White and his men would have found graves and dead bodies, as well as reports detailing this slow, painful death. For the same reasons, it's doubtful that they died of disease or a fatal epidemic, such as influenza or smallpox.

Bad relations with the neighboring Native people might have become worse, and local tribes may have killed or kidnapped the settlers. Or they may have been attacked by Spanish soldiers who came up from Florida. Some people theorized that they built a boat or paid a trading ship to sail them back to England but were lost at sea.

Historians who study Native Americans have suggested the settlers moved in with a neighboring tribe called the Chowanoc. A report written in 1612 describes Native settlements with two-story houses that had stone walls. This was the English style of building, so some historians and anthropologists (people who study humans' traditions, beliefs, and relationships to their environment) think the lost colonists likely taught the Native people how to build them. The same report mentions sightings of Europeans at Native settlements.

LOST ARMY OF CAMBYSES

The people of the Lost Colony aren't the only large group to have vanished. Legends from more than 2,500 years ago tell of an army of 50,000 Persian soldiers fighting for King Cambyses against Egypt. The men were halfway across an Egyptian desert when a huge sandstorm suddenly swirled up. Thousands of soldiers were buried without a trace.

Many historians believe the story is a myth, but geologists and Egyptologists (people who study ancient Egypt) have searched for evidence of the soldiers for many years. Some researchers claim to have found human remains, tools, and weapons in the desert that date back to the time of the Persian army. However, their finds have not been verified. In 2014, a Dutch Egyptologist deciphered an inscription that

he believes states the Persian army was defeated and the sandstorm story was a cover-up to explain why the soldiers were never seen again.

DEADLY INTRIGUE AT COURT

There's a more sinister possibility that some historians have suggested concerning the fate of the Lost Colony. Sir Walter Raleigh, who had financed the Roanoke Island venture, was a favorite with Queen Elizabeth. That gave him a lot of power—and also earned him the jealousy and resentment of many in the English court. There were likely people so eager to hurt his reputation that they were even willing to sabotage his colony in the New World and the people trying to survive there.

One of Raleigh's biggest enemies in the English court was Sir Francis Walsingham, a top official and statesman. It just happened that years earlier, when Raleigh's captain Simon Fernandez had been about to hang for piracy, his life had been saved—by Walsingham. It's not hard to imagine that he would have done anything Walsingham asked him to do, even harm innocent settlers. And as pilot of their ship, he would have had the opportunity.

When Fernandez dropped the settlers at Roanoke, he claimed the voyage to the New World had taken too long and there wasn't time for him to carry them on to Chesapeake Bay. This original destination was only a few days away, so it seems like a pretty flimsy excuse. Fernandez may have had orders from Walsingham to drop Raleigh's colonists at Roanoke, since it was more dangerous—thanks to the earlier

Sir Francis Walsingham was known as Queen Elizabeth I's "spymaster." He gathered information from across Europe for the queen.

British soldiers' arrogance and brutality toward the Native people.

Raleigh's enemies in England may have helped delay White from returning to Roanoke with supplies, which further sabotaged the settlement. These enemies may also have spread the story that the colonists were dead, so that the English government would see no point in spending time and money looking for them.

JUST REALLY BAD TIMING

What likely happened to the Lost Colony is that when the settlers' food ran out, friendly Native people in the area brought the colonists to their villages to live with them. What scientists proved for certain in 1998 is that the Roanoke colonists could hardly have picked a worse time to try to build a settlement.

By studying tree rings of ancient trees in the area, scientists showed that from 1587 to 1589, there was a major dry spell in North Carolina, the worst drought in 800 years. The rings during this period were unusually narrow and thin. That meant while White was in England, the Roanoke colonists had almost no fresh water for drinking or

A tree's rings, or growth rings, can give scientists a good idea of how old the tree is. They also tell a lot about the environment and climate changes where the tree grew.

watering their crops. Perhaps disaster struck the colony before the people could find a way to move to the mainland, with its freshwater lakes and rivers.

Other professors and researchers in early American history say the colonists' timing may have been deadly for another reason. During this period, the Native people who got along with the colonists were losing control of this area of North Carolina. They were being replaced by Native tribes who were hostile to the English. The male settlers may have been killed and the women and children captured as slaves.

THE CLUE OF THE LUMBEE TRIBE

Many digs have been conducted on Roanoke Island, but no definite evidence of the Lost Colony has ever been found. Croatoan, the island where White thought the colonists had gone, is believed to be today's Hatteras Island, about 80 kilometers (50 miles) south of Roanoke. After more than 400 years, it may be almost impossible to find any traces of the settlers on either island. The ocean level has risen as much as 400 meters (1,312 feet) in the last 400 years. So the site of the Lost Colony and any clues it contains are likely deep under water.

The Lumbee (the name means "dark water" in Algonquian) tribe that lives in the area may hold a clue to the Lost Colony's fate. The Lumbee are descendants of the Croatoans, the Lost Colony's neighbors. The Lumbee began to appear about 50 years after the Lost Colony disappeared. They were described as speaking English and having European features such as light hair and fair skin.

There are many sand dunes on Hatteras Island, which was once known as Croatoan Island. Today the area is known for its fishing and surfing.

Today, in the town of Pembroke, North Carolina, there are more than 40 families with the same last names as the lost colonists and who are part Native American and part European.

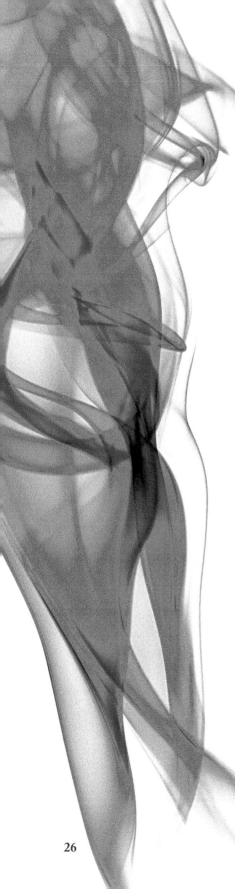

DNA ACROSS THE OCEAN

DNA (deoxyribonucleic acid) testing may be able to show if there's a definite connection between the Lumbee and the lost colonists, but currently, the process is too expensive to test everyone. More research needs to be done to target the people who are most likely to be descendants.

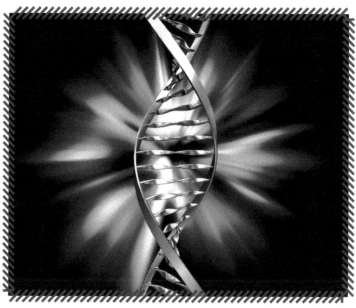

DNA (above) is the blueprint of genetic material that your cells receive from your parents and that makes you unique. If a descendant of the lost colonists living in England today can be shown to have similar DNA to someone in the United States who is known to be a descendant of early American settlers, then a connection to the Lost Colony is likely. It would mean that at least some of the colonists must have survived, and that it just might be possible to trace what happened to them.

Roanoke's governor John White was also an artist. This picture of Native people in North Carolina was based on one of his drawings.

HUNTING RELICS

It would be handy for researchers investigating the Lost Colony to know how English people from the late 1500s lived: what they ate, for instance, and how they buried their dead. As well, a knowledge of the culture of Native Americans living in North Carolina at that time could give historians insights into how they might have treated the newcomers.

It's important for researchers to have in-depth knowledge about civilizations, cultures, and communities so they can determine which are the most likely sites of relics and artifacts. For instance, people searching for old coins—it's called coin shooting—need to know the location of ghost towns or places where small towns sprang up and then disappeared. As well, it helps to know that people used to bury money and jewelry in their backyards in case their houses were robbed or burned down. Sometimes those valuables are still there, just waiting to be dug up.

This is John White's map of the Virginia and North Carolina coastline. Roanoke is the small, oval-shaped island in the middle of the map to the right. Some people believe the patch on the map near the middle left, between the letter "I" and the ship, covers a symbol for a settlement. The other patch is in the lower middle, along the coast.

DOES THE MAP HOLD THE SECRET?

One of the best clues about what happened to the Lost Colony was discovered in 2012. Experts reexamined a map that Governor John White drew more than 400 years ago and discovered it held new information. The details had been ignored for so long because they were hidden under paper patches on the image. One of the patches concealed a symbol at the mouth of the Chowan River on North Carolina's coast. Some historians identified the symbol as a settlement.

In 2012, archaeologist Nicholas M. Luccketti and his crew began excavating the area indicated by the settlement symbol— they called it Site X. The searchers revealed in August 2015 that they found a type of pottery that was used by colonists only before 1606. "We have evidence from this site," says Luccketti, "that strongly indicates that there were Roanoke colonists here."

Other crews had continued searching for evidence of the Lost Colony on Hatteras Island, once known as Croatoan Island. It's a narrow island, but is one of the longest islands in the mainland United States, measuring almost 80 kilometers (50 miles) in length.

In 2015, archaeologists found on the island what looked like a wooden board for writing on, as well as the metal hilt of a sword. Researchers believe the two sets of finds suggest the colonists split up, but their fate is still unknown.

John White died, haunted by the mystery of the colonists' disappearance. If he had been allowed to return immediately to Roanoke, the colonists might have been saved. But thanks to White and his map, and to modern technology, the Lost Colony may eventually be located.

STATE-OF-THE-ART SEARCHES

Historians and scientists continue to search for the Lost Colony. Thanks to new technology, they hope to find clues that will solve the mystery of the settlers' disappearance.

A magnetometer is one instrument that has been used to try to find the Lost Colony. This tool detects iron and magnetic material, and measures the direction of the magnetic field. It can detect changes in the field caused by buried objects, such as cannons, nails, and muskets, even if they're down as deep as 4 meters (13 feet).

Researchers are also using ground-penetrating radar (GPR), which emits radio waves into the ground, then measures the echo as the signal bounces off anything buried underground. With this technology,

A magnetometer can be mounted at the front of a helicopter to allow researchers to easily examine large areas for magnetic material.

researchers can identify if there is anything below the surface, so they know where to dig.

Another technology scientists use to locate buried artifacts is Lidar. It's similar to radar, but it emits and receives light instead of radio waves. This technology measures distance by aiming a laser on a target, then analyzing the light that's reflected—the name comes from the words "light" and "radar."

Lidar allows researchers to make detailed maps of archaeological sites, even if they're covered with grass and trees. Lidar can reveal features that can't be seen from the ground or through aerial photography.

Metal detectors use magnetic fields to pinpoint metal buried underground. With computer technology, searchers can alter the sensitivity of the machine to identify the kind of metal they have located.

The Global Positioning System (GPS), which uses a satellite navigation system to provide location information, gives modern researchers information about search sites before they even leave their computers.

This GPR machinery is very portable.

As well as helping scientists locate buried objects, Lidar scans allow engineers to examine dams for damage.

FRANKLIN EXPEDITION

HIDDEN IN ICE AND SNOW

"Permission to approach the bridge, Captain," said the first mate.

"Granted," muttered the captain, not taking the spyglass from his eye.

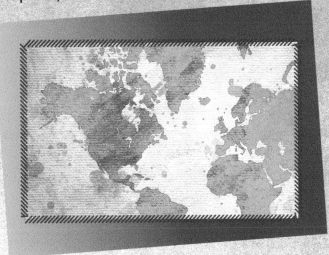

"Captain," said the first mate hesitantly, wringing his hands, "we've been searching for months, and there's no sign of Sir John and his ships."

"Go on," said the captain.

"The men are getting nervous," continued the first mate. "Winter is coming and our ship could get frozen in, any day. Supplies are running low. We've got to give up the search."

"Tarnation!" cursed the captain, slamming his fist against the ship's railing. "We have looked everywhere for Franklin and his ships. We've searched every cussed island from Beechey and Somerset to Prince of Wales and King William. Where can Franklin's ships be?"

The first mate remained silent.

"All right," agreed the captain, his shoulders slumping in defeat. "We turn around at daybreak and make for England."

"Thank you, sir. The men will be much relieved. And may God have mercy on the souls of all those brave men lost in this frozen wilderness."

"But can you tell me," the captain said, gazing out over the vast icy landscape, "how the most modern ships in Her Majesty's navy and the expert captain and crew aboard them could vanish without a trace?"

ARCTIC-BOUND

In the spring of 1845, crowds gathered in Greenhithe, on the southeast coast of England, to cheer as the great explorer Sir John Franklin sailed off on his latest glorious expedition. The famous explorer and his crew were setting out aboard the HMS *Erebus* and the HMS *Terror* (HMS stands for "Her Majesty's Ship") to become the first ships to sail the complete length of the Northwest Passage. This was the sea route through the Arctic Ocean, over the top of Canada, that connected the Atlantic and Pacific Oceans and would allow ships to save months in their journeys to Asia.

Rear-Admiral Sir John Franklin. Even when he was a young boy, he loved the sea joining the British Royal Navy when he was just 14 years old.

Thick ice and harsh conditions had caused other expeditions to fail in their endeavors to sail the route. But Franklin's expedition was well equipped with the latest technology. This included steam engines and a steam-based heating system that would keep the crew warm and provide fresh water for the engines' boilers. Also new was a mechanism for pulling the ships' rudders and propellers up into iron wells to protect them from being damaged by ice or rocks. Franklin had bigger plans than just sailing the length of the Northwest Passage. He was determined to map all the Arctic islands and explore a land never seen by Europeans.

Lady Jane Franklin sadly bid her husband farewell. But like everyone in England, she expected he and his men would take no more than a year to conquer the icy passage.

No one could have guessed that neither the ships nor the crew would ever return.

THE SEARCH FOR THE NORTHWEST PASSAGE

By the 1450s, Europeans had been trading with India and China for gold, silk, and spices for hundreds of years. The route the traders took through what is now Afghanistan and Iran became known as the Silk Road. The journey was long and dangerous.

Around 1350, European traders began to wonder if it was possible to sail to China. They had no idea that entire continents—North and South America—lay between them and Asia. They soon realized they would have to look for a route over the top of what is now Canada: the Northwest Passage.

Norwegian explorer Roald Amundsen captained a ship through the Northwest Passage in 1905, although his expedition spent two winters stuck in the ice at King William Island. The first passage completed in one season was in 1944, by Norwegian-Canadian Henry A. Larsen and the *St. Roch*, a Royal Canadian Mounted Police ship.

The trails that made up the Silk Road were beautiful and winding—and treacherous.

A LIFE AT SEA

Franklin was an experienced captain who had been at sea for most of his life. He sailed as far away as Australia and took part in so many battles that he was partially deaf from the noise of gunfire.

In 1819, Franklin led an expedition to map the north coast of Canada. More than half his crew died, most of starvation. They were so desperate for food that they tried to eat their own leather boots, earning Franklin the nickname "the man who ate his boots." British people were thrilled by the stories of the horrible journey, and Franklin's skill at commanding crews and ships was praised. He returned to England in 1822 and was made a captain in the Royal Navy.

Franklin was back in the Arctic from 1825 to 1827. He and his men mapped the coastline and studied the rocks and minerals of the area, as well as the plants. Thanks to his many successful Arctic expeditions, and to his adventures and narrow escapes, he was considered a hero.

Franklin was knighted in 1829. Britain lost interest in exploring the North for the next 20 years, but Franklin wanted to keep busy. In 1836, he was appointed lieutenant governor of Van Diemen's Land, which is today's Tasmania, an island off the southeast coast of Australia.

When Franklin returned to England in 1843, a little less than 500 kilometers (310 miles) of Arctic coastline remained unexplored. Franklin was already 59 years old, but when the British government offered him the chance to return to the Arctic and complete the mapping of the Northwest Passage, Franklin was eager to become an explorer again.

HIGH-TECH SHIPS

Franklin's ships were outfitted with the most modern inventions. The HMS *Erebus* (named after the Greek god of darkness, associated with the underworld) and the HMS *Terror* were bomb vessels and had taken part in a number of naval battles, so they were strongly built. These ships were constructed to withstand the jarring recoil of their mortars (a type of cannon), so they had strong, thick internal wooden frameworks.

The ships had reinforced steel plates on the bow (front) and hull (bottom) of the boat so they could break through ice. They were heated with steam, and had steam engines to help power the ship through ice-blocked waters. The iron rudder (a blade at the back of a ship used to change its direction) and propeller could

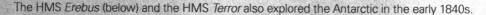

The HMS *Erebus* (below) and the HMS *Terror* also explored the Antarctic in the early 1840s.

be drawn into an iron-lined well to keep them from being damaged by the thick sheets of ice.

Franklin knew how grueling the expedition would be, so he made sure he and his 129-man crew were well prepared. They took three years' worth of supplies, including 8,000 cans of meat, soup, and vegetables. Putting food in tin cans to preserve it had only been done for about 30 years, and Franklin wanted everything about the expedition to be modern. But the contract to supply the food was given to a cheap supplier who had only a few months to assemble it all. That haste would prove fatal to Franklin and his men.

The ships were also loaded with lots of lemon juice to prevent scurvy, a disease caused by a lack of vitamin C. Scurvy causes high fever, bleeding, and eventually death due to heart failure, so it's very important to avoid it. Franklin even included a piano, more than 1,000 books, and fine crystal drinking glasses. There were three pets on board: a cat, a monkey, and a Newfoundland dog.

The expedition was spotted on July 26, 1845, by a British whaling ship off the north end of Baffin Island—and there are no written records of them ever being seen again. How could the largest, best-equipped expedition that the British Royal Navy had ever assembled to explore the Arctic disappear?

Many explorers took Newfoundland dogs with them. This large dog is especially good at rescuing people from the water because of its strength, thick double coat, and ability to swim well.

More than 200 years before Franklin headed off in search of the Northwest Passage, Henry Hudson sailed from England to find a route through the Arctic. His voyages in 1607, 1608, and 1609 were all unsuccessful, but Hudson kept trying.

In April 1610, with a ship financed by England, Hudson set out again to try to find the Northwest Passage. By September, he was lost in what he thought was a huge sea. His ship was stuck in the ice for the winter and the crew barely survived. They mutinied in June and set Hudson, his son, and a few other sailors adrift in a small boat. Neither Hudson nor any of those men were ever seen again, although the "sea" where he was lost was named after him: Hudson Bay.

HENRY HUDSON,

Henry Hudson is still famous today because his exploration of North America led to the development of the fur trade. Many European countries became very interested in the New World because of this.

TRAPPED

Based on reports by Inuit hunters, Franklin and his men spent the winter of 1845–46 in a sheltered area by Beechey Island, north of Baffin Island. The crew had tried to break the ice around the ship to create a path and allow it to move, but by early fall 1845, the ice was already over 2 meters (7 feet) deep, much too thick for the ship to break through.

Some of the men tried to shoot birds or hunt other animals to add to their rations. Others packed snow blocks around the stationary ship to add a layer of insulation. They had no way to communicate with the rest of the world but tried to keep busy with exercise, music, reading, and chores.

Franklin's ship HMS *Terror* was one of Britain's battleships in the War of 1812. From 1836 to 1848, the ship sailed Arctic and Antarctic waters in a number of expeditions. In 1837, it was damaged by the Arctic ice (shown here).

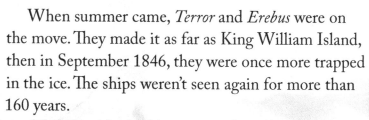

When summer came, *Terror* and *Erebus* were on the move. They made it as far as King William Island, then in September 1846, they were once more trapped in the ice. The ships weren't seen again for more than 160 years.

After Franklin had been gone for two years, Lady Franklin was sure something was wrong and she begged the British Royal Navy to send out an expedition to find her husband. But the navy officials were in no hurry because they knew the *Erebus* and the *Terror* had been outfitted with enough food to last three years.

As well, in those days, not hearing from people for months or even years wasn't unusual because there was no e-mail, telephones, or international mail system like we have today. So the navy waited until 1848 before assigning any ships to the task of searching for Franklin.

Eventually, Britain sent more than 40 expeditions to find the Franklin group. At that time, it took a ship from England about two months just to reach the top of Canada. At one point, ten British ships and two American boats were all heading to the Arctic to join in the search. Most of the searchers never saw a single trace of the lost men and those two high-tech ships.

Although there'd been no word from anyone in the expedition, many people still believed Franklin was alive, and in 1852, he was given a promotion in the navy. But two years later, in 1854, the British government declared that the great Arctic explorer and his crew had died in the service of their monarch, Queen Victoria. However, their actual fate remained an icy mystery.

LADY FRANKLIN'S LAMENT

Lady Jane Franklin paid for seven expeditions to search for her husband or his records. She even traveled to Out Stack, which is the most northern of all the British Isles, since it was as close as she could get to her missing husband. She also supported many other expeditions, which kept her husband and his mysterious fate in the news.

Even when she received the sad news, from the note in the cairn, (see page 49) that Franklin was dead, she encouraged searchers to continue looking for his written records. She died in 1875 before the last expedition she sponsored returned to England.

Many stories and songs have been written about Lady Franklin's devotion to her husband. One of the most famous is called "Lady Franklin's Lament"—you can listen to it online.

Lady Franklin was a well-educated, determined woman. Her many efforts to discover the fate of her husband greatly added to the world's knowledge of the Arctic.

The British government offered a reward of 20,000 pounds to anyone who rescued Franklin and his crew. That would be worth more than $1 million in today's dollars.

£20,000
REWARD

WILL BE GIVEN BY

Her Majesty's Government

TO ANY PARTY OR PARTIES, OF ANY COUNTRY, WHO SHALL RENDER EFFICIENT
ASSISTANCE TO THE CREWS OF THE

DISCOVERY SHIPS

UNDER THE COMMAND OF

SIR JOHN FRANKLIN,

1.—To any Party or Parties who, in the judgment of the Board of Admiralty, shall discover and effectually relieve the Crews of Her Majesty's Ships "Erebus" and "Terror," the

£20,000.

OR

2.—To any Party or Parties who, in the judgment of the Board of Admiralty, shall discover and effectually relieve *any* of the Crews of Her Majesty's Ships "Erebus" and "Terror," or shall convey such intelligence as shall lead to the relief of such Crews or *any* of them, the Sum of

£10,000.

OR

3.—To any Party or Parties who, in the judgment of the Board of Admiralty, shall by virtue of his or their efforts first succeed in ascertaining their fate,

£10,000.

W. A. B. HAMILTON,

Admiralty, March 7th, 1850.

Secretary of the Admiralty.

VANISHED

HMS *INVESTIGATOR*

Far more ships and sailors were lost looking for Franklin's vanished expedition than were in the original expedition. One of these ships was the HMS *Investigator.* She was purchased and fitted specifically to search for the Franklin group. Timber was added to her upper deck to help it bear the snow and ice loads, and iron and steel plates were attached to help push through the ice.

The *Investigator* sailed to the Arctic in 1848 and again in 1850. In 1853, the *Investigator* was trapped in fast-forming ice that cut them off from open water. The crew was rescued by a Royal Navy sled team and taken to another ship, and the *Investigator* was abandoned. It wasn't until 2010 that her wreckage was found. In July 2011, divers took photos that showed the wreck was in good condition, likely because the cold arctic water slowed down deterioration.

DID THE INUIT HAVE THE ANSWERS?

In 1854, Scottish explorer Dr. John Rae was surveying the Boothia Peninsula, south of Somerset Island, for the Hudson's Bay Company. He realized how much the Inuit people knew about surviving in the North: they could read the landscape, and they knew a great deal about what was happening around them. Most British explorers ignored the Inuit, assuming they couldn't be helpful, but Rae questioned them to see if they knew anything about Franklin's fate.

The Inuit told Rae that both of Franklin's ships had become stuck in the ice. The crew eventually decided to abandon the ships and walk to safety. But by this point, they were weak with hunger—they refused to

When the Inuit were out hunting, they noticed many details about their environment. They knew a lot about Franklin and his crew, and passed on the information to explorer Dr. John Rae.

eat raw seal meat as the Inuit did—and were trying to pull heavy sleds full of supplies. In their thin canvas boots and wool jackets, rather than thick furs and skins as the Inuit wore, the men died of the cold, not one of them completing the trek.

The first kayak was used more than 4,000 years ago. The skin on a kayak is smooth and flexible so it glides silently through the Arctic waters.

RADICAL JOHN RAE

Dr. John Rae was the first British explorer to learn details about the fate of the Franklin expedition. In 1854, he interviewed Inuit hunters who said that both of Franklin's ships had been frozen in the ice. Unlike many of the British explorers, Rae respected the Inuit and learned survival techniques from them.

Rather than being pleased to receive news of Franklin's fate, the British shunned Rae because he reported something else the Inuit had told him: the starving men of Franklin's expedition had eaten their already dead companions.

In July 2015, researchers from Canada and Britain analyzed the bones of some of the crew. They found knife marks on the bones and noticed the bones looked polished. That indicated that they'd been heated in water, a technique used to extract marrow. The scientists' findings confirmed that Rae and the Inuit had been right.

THE CLUE IN THE CAIRN

Lady Franklin was desperate to discover more about the fate of her husband, so she financed her own expeditions and supported other searches by providing money and offering rewards. She even pressured the government to send out more searchers.

In 1857, Lady Franklin hired Captain Francis Leopold McClintock to search for her husband. When he reached King William Island, he met Inuit who had silver cutlery and buttons with markings that identified them as belonging to the Franklin expedition. The hunters told of two ships that had been crushed in the ice and of seeing sailors who "fell down and died as they walked."

Franklin and his men battled against the Arctic's harsh environment. Some died as they struggled through the snow.

On the island's south coast, McClintock found a human skeleton, still dressed in a shredded steward's uniform. Then, to the north, McClintock found a rock cairn (a marker made of a pile of stones) that held a tin container inside it, with a single piece of paper in it. The paper was dated May 23, 1847, and described how the expedition had spent its first winter at Beechey Island, then its second winter off the coast of King William Island.

But written around the edges of the paper was another note. It reported that Franklin's ships had been trapped in ice since September 12, 1846. The crew had left the ships on April 26, 1848. The note stated that 24 of the crew had died. That included their leader, John Franklin, who died on June 11, 1847. You can take a look at the note yourself, on page 59.

From 1848 to 1859, Francis Leopold McClintock took part in expeditions to find Franklin and his ships.

The note described how the remaining crew of 105 planned to walk south to Black River, then row to the nearest fur-trading fort. But the walking took them much longer than they anticipated—pulling heavy sleds full of supplies would have slowed them down greatly. At some point, the party split up, with the weakest men heading back to the ship to await rescue and the others pressing on in a desperate attempt to get help. None of them ever reached their destination.

McClintock and his men found a lifeboat from the expedition, mounted on a sled. Inside the boat, they made the grisly discovery of two human skeletons. Also in the boat, propped against the side, were two

Unlike many other Arctic explorers, Francis Leopold McClintock respected the Inuit and their ways. He and his men wore Inuit-style parkas and used sled dogs.

loaded guns. Perhaps they'd been set up to be fired to attract the attention of any rescuers. But rescue had never come.

The findings of McClintock and his men proved that when the Franklin expedition survivors completed their final march, they walked across the last unmapped gap in the Northwest Passage. The expedition had succeeded, but it had cost all the men their lives.

BURIED IN THE ICE

In 1984, anthropologist Owen Beattie and his assistants traveled to Beechey Island to try to solve the mystery of what had caused the death of Franklin's crew. An anthropologist is a scientist who studies people, both their culture and their biological characteristics.

Beattie and his crew dug up a coffin from a grave on the island to examine the body of the sailor inside. The blistering cold had kept it startlingly well preserved. The body, belonging to John Torrington, was more than 130 years old, yet still had hair, skin, and eyelashes.

An artist imagined what explorers might find when they discovered the graves of Franklin and his crew. When a coffin was finally opened in 1984, its contents were even more amazing.

Bad weather closed in and the researchers had to stop work and leave the site. They carefully reburied Torrington, but returned in 1986 to investigate two other graves of Franklin's crew. One of the bodies they examined belonged to Able Seaman John Hartnell—his great-great nephew was the photographer for the researchers. The scientists took samples of Hartnell's hair, bone, and other tissue in hopes of discovering what chemicals and substances the men might have eaten or breathed in. The researchers also removed samples from the third sailor, William Braine. Then they carefully reburied the bodies in their icy arctic graves.

DEADLY DINNER

In 1987, when Beattie received the lab results on his samples, they showed the men had suffered from acute lead poisoning. This illness would have made them sick and weak, but also likely affected their minds, causing them to act strangely. It would have been hard for them to think clearly or make good decisions.

Tin cans, such as this one found on Beechey Island, were an important clue about the fate of the Franklin expedition.

Franklin's expedition had carried thousands of cans of food. But preserving food in tin cans was a new technology in the 1840s and the workers who had prepared the tins for Franklin's expedition had been pressed for time.

When Beattie studied the tin-can fragments he had collected at Beechey Island, he found that the cans had been sloppily sealed on the inside with far too much solder made from melted lead and tin. The large chunks of solder had dissolved into the food, quickly filling it with high levels of lead.

Beattie's research proved that the lead in the sailors' bodies and the lead in the tin cans was the same. No wonder that in the 1890s, the British government prohibited soldering on the inside of food cans.

In January 2014, Scottish scientists suggested that the high amount of lead in the sailors' bodies may have been normal for the British population of the day. In Britain in the 1800s, water flowed into homes through lead pipes. There was a lot of lead in the air and in the food, and lead poisoning happened often. Lead poisoning was definitely one of the factors that led to the death of Franklin and his men, but there may have been others.

It's true that some of the men likely died of scurvy, cold, or malnutrition. Beattie's investigations also proved that Hartnell died of tuberculosis (a lung disease) or pneumonia. But lead poisoning had undoubtedly weakened or killed Franklin's crew.

How could the men have died of scurvy when Franklin brought along so much lemon juice to combat it? In fact, the juice packed for the expedition probably did the crew little good. Experts now think that the juice went bad in less than a year and had to be thrown away.

EXTREME DISAPPEARANCES

In attempts to conquer new and extreme territories, many explorers have vanished. In 1911, Roald Amundsen became the first explorer to reach the South Pole. But he disappeared in the Arctic in 1928 while flying on a rescue mission. Despite many searches, including by unmanned submarines in 2004 and 2009, no trace of Amundsen's plane has ever been found.

George Mallory and Andrew Irvine attempted to climb Mount Everest in 1924 but disappeared close to the summit. For years, there was no trace of the pair. Then in 1999, Mallory's frozen remains were found by the Mallory and Irvine Research Expedition.

In 2010, using a computer-assembled montage of aerial photos, a team of Everest historians believed it had located Irvine's body, though it has not yet confirmed this. If Mallory and Irvine made it to Everest's summit before they died, they would have been the first climbers to accomplish this feat.

Mount Everest is the highest mountain in the world.
No one officially reached the summit until 1953.

TOO PROUD TO SUCCEED?

Pride may also have led to the deaths of Franklin and his men. They believed that their British ways were the best and most advanced. They wouldn't eat seal meat—which prevented scurvy—like the Inuit did. They also refused to dress in furs or use dogs (instead of men) to pull sleds, which would have helped them conserve energy.

Seal meat was an important part of the Inuit diet during Franklin's time. It's lean meat that's high in iron, B vitamins, and other nutrients. It could be dried for storage and eaten when food was scarce.

    The British seamen could have learned practical and effective ways to survive in the North if they had only listened to the Inuits' advice. Perhaps then some of them might have survived their dreadful ordeal.

FAR BELOW THE ICY WAVES

For years, the Inuit had told Arctic explorers and researchers stories of ships lying in the water off Hat Island, a small island southwest of King William Island. In September 2014, almost 170 years since the ships were last seen, researchers using a robotic underwater vehicle

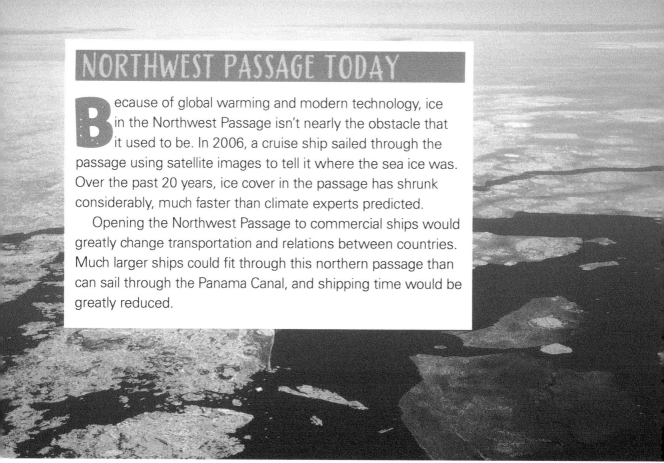

NORTHWEST PASSAGE TODAY

Because of global warming and modern technology, ice in the Northwest Passage isn't nearly the obstacle that it used to be. In 2006, a cruise ship sailed through the passage using satellite images to tell it where the sea ice was. Over the past 20 years, ice cover in the passage has shrunk considerably, much faster than climate experts predicted.

Opening the Northwest Passage to commercial ships would greatly change transportation and relations between countries. Much larger ships could fit through this northern passage than can sail through the Panama Canal, and shipping time would be greatly reduced.

During summer in the Arctic, the sea ice breaks up and ships can sail through the Northwest Passage.

discovered the wreckage of a ship that was identified as one of Franklin's two vessels. The next month, the remains were identified as the *Erebus*. It's believed the ships sank because the ice cracked their wooden timbers.

Despite their high-tech equipment, researchers faced many challenges when searching for the Franklin ships. Much of the Arctic Ocean has never been mapped, so little is known about the ocean floor. As well, for many years, the open-water season in the Arctic was just a few months in the summer, so it was hard to search effectively. Climate change has meant that the icy ocean stays open for longer stretches, allowing researchers more time to study the area.

NEVER GIVE UP

In November 2014, a brass bell was recovered from the *Erebus*. Embossed on it is the date 1845—the year Franklin and his men set out—as well as symbols marking the bell as property of the British government. Divers also found cannons, pulley blocks, and ropes at the site, but left them in place since moving them out of their cold environment could cause damage.

The "broad arrow" on this bell (top) identifies the bell as property of the British government. An underwater archaeologist is measuring the muzzle of a cannon (bottom).

Also in the fall of 2014, an iron fitting from one of Franklin's ships and two broad arrows were found on land near where the *Erebus* was located. It's possible more artifacts will provide solutions to the many questions about the ill-fated expedition, such as where Franklin's body lies and what happened during the last days of the expedition.

Since Franklin's body has never been found, the exact cause of his death remains a mystery. Although the *Erebus* has been discovered, as well as the graves on Beechey Island, there is one more important thing that is still missing: Franklin's records of his expedition.

Dr. John Rae, who was the first to discover any solid leads about what had happened to Franklin and his men, suggested the Inuit destroyed the records. According to him, the northern people had a fear of paper with writing on it. If they had found Franklin's records, they may have burned them. Or Franklin's last words could have simply disintegrated in the wind and snow. The Arctic doesn't give up its secrets easily, so the brave captain's records may have vanished forever.

THE NOTE IN THE CAIRN

On the facing page is the note from Franklin's crew that Captain McClintock found in 1859. It is a standard British Admiralty form. Part of the message is repeated at the bottom in (from top to bottom) French, Spanish, Dutch, Danish, and German. Two messages were handwritten on the form. The first message, printed at the top of the form, says:

H.M. Ships Erebus and Terror
28 of May 1847 Wintered in the Ice in Lat. 70°5'N Long. 98°.23'W Having wintered in 1846-7 at Beechey Island in Lat 74°43'28"N Long 91°39'15"W After having ascended Wellington Channel to Lat 77° and returned by the West side of Cornwallis Island. Sir John Franklin commanding the Expedition. All well

The dates the message states for wintering at Beechey Island are wrong, likely because the message was written from memory and the writer was probably suffering from starvation and possibly lead poisoning. The expedition actually spent the winters of 1845–47 at Beechey Island. At the bottom, the handwriting says:

Party consisting of 2 Officers and 6 Men left the ships on Monday 24th May 1847.—Gm. Gore, Lieut., Chas. F. DesVoeux, Mate

On the left side of the form is a second, later message. Some of it is now missing, but what's there says:

25th April 1848 HM Ships Terror and Erebus were deserted on the 22nd April 5 leagues NNW of this having been beset since 12th Sept 1846. The officers and crews consisting of 105 souls under the command of Captain F. R. M. Crozier landed here—in Lat. 69°37'42" Long. 98°41' This paper was found by Lt. Irving under the cairn supposed to have

The message continues on the right side of the form, near the bottom:

been built by Sir James Ross in 1831— 4 miles to the Northward—where it had been deposited by the late Commander Gore June [May is scratched out by the writer] 1847. Sir James Ross' pillar has not however been found and the paper has been transferred to this position which is that in which Sir J. Ross' pillar was erected—Sir John Franklin died on the 11th of June 1847 and the total loss by deaths in the Expedition has been to this date 9 officers and 15 men.—James Fitzjames Captain HMS Erebus F. R. M. Crozier Captain & Senior Offr And start on tomorrow 26th for Backs Fish River

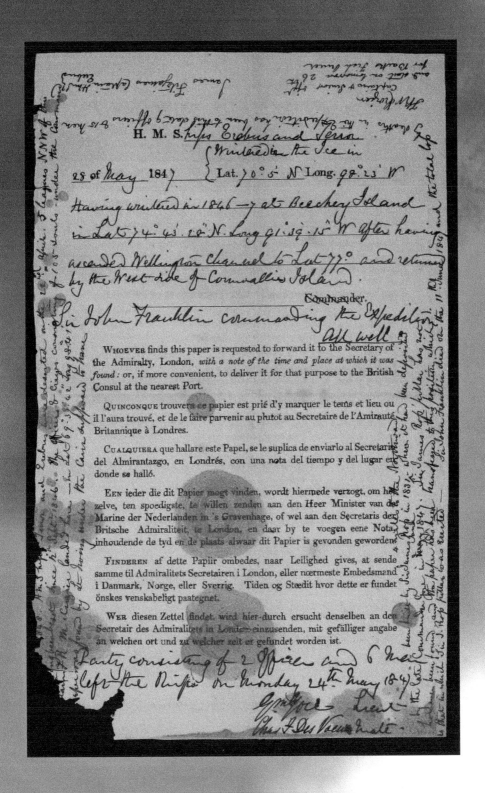

H. M. S. ships Erebus and Terror
Wintered in the Ice in
28 of May 1847 Lat. 70° 5' N Long. 98°.23' W

Having wintered in 1846—7 at Beechey Island
in Lat 74° 43' 28" N. Long 91°39'.15" W after having
ascended Wellington Channel to Lat 77° and returned
by the West side of Cornwallis Island.

Sir John Franklin commanding the Expedition

Commander

All well

WHOEVER finds this paper is requested to forward it to the Secretary of the Admiralty, London, *with a note of the time and place at which it was found*: or, if more convenient, to deliver it for that purpose to the British Consul at the nearest Port.

QUINCONQUE trouvera ce papier est prié d'y marquer le tems et lieu ou il l'aura trouvé, et de le faire parvenir au plutot au Secretaire de l'Amirauté Britannique à Londres.

CUALQUIERA que hallare este Papel, se le suplica de enviarlo al Secretario del Almirantazgo, en Londrés, con una nota del tiempo y del lugar en donde se halló.

EEN ieder die dit Papier mogt vinden, wordt hiermede verzogt, om het zelve, ten spoedigste, te willen zenden aan den Heer Minister van de Marine der Nederlanden in 's Gravenhage, of wel aan den Secretaris der Britsche Admiraliteit, te London, en daar by te voegen eene Nota, inhoudende de tyd en de plaats alwaar dit Papier is gevonden geworden.

FINDEREN af dette Papiir ombedes, naar Leilighed gives, at sende samme til Admiralitets Secretairen i London, eller nærmeste Embedsmand i Danmark, Norge, eller Sverrig. Tiden og Stædit hvor dette er fundet önskes venskabeligt paategnet.

WER diesen Zettel findet, wird hier-durch ersucht denselben an den Secretair des Admiralitets in London einzusenden, mit gefälliger angabe an welchen ort und zu welcher zeit er gefundet worden ist.

Party consisting of 2 Officers and 6 Men
left the Ships on Monday 24th May 1847.

Gore Lieut
Chas F Des Voeux mate

FOUND: ONE SHIP!

The underwater robot the scientists used to search for Franklin's ships is called an autonomous underwater vehicle (AUV). These programmable vehicles can dive, drift, or glide through the water. They either communicate with their operators constantly using satellite signals or only at regular intervals.

With sensors such as sonars (to locate underwater objects by echolocation) and magnetometers (to detect iron or magnetic materials), AUVs can provide information about undersea areas where it's too difficult or dangerous for humans to dive. In addition to searching for ancient shipwrecks, these robots can be used to discover the wreckage of planes that have crashed at sea. Some are solar powered and even tweet their findings on Twitter!

To survey the ocean floor, scientists use high-tech multibeam sonar and side-scan sonar. Many sonar devices send out one focused beam of sound

This autonomous underwater vehicle (AUV) has buried object scanning sonar (BOSS) located in its two "wings."

The AUV shown here can cover a large area underwater, take photos, and collect data and samples. It can monitor areas over long periods.

to map the small area of the seafloor that's directly below the ship. The sonar machine transmits sound energy and analyzes the return signal (or echo) that bounces back off the ocean floor and any objects lying there.

Multibeam sonars allow researchers to examine an area of ocean floor that's many kilometers wide. Thousands of measurements of the depth of the water are collected every few seconds with this instrument to create a rainbow-colored map showing ocean depth and objects lying on the ocean floor.

With a side-scan sonar, the transmitted energy forms into a fan shape to sweep the ocean floor from either side of the ship it's in. This system produces images that look like black-and-white photographs and are especially useful for detecting objects on the ocean floor. They can't show how deep the water is, but are often used with regular sonar and multibeam sonar to create a full image of a section of the ocean.

What secrets might scientists find aboard the *Erebus*? The high-tech equipment has shown that the deck looks to be in fairly good shape. That means the contents of the ship should be well preserved. As well, the *Terror* is likely nearby and may contain the answers to more of the mysteries that have surrounded the Franklin expedition for so long. Searchers may finally discover what killed Sir John Franklin or why the crew eventually abandoned the ships.

This AUV can move slowly over the seafloor or hover in place. It can flash a strobe light, then snap a photo every few seconds.

MARY CELESTE

LEGENDARY GHOST SHIP

"All right, keep your eyes wide open and shout if you discover anything suspicious," said First Mate Oliver Deveau. "We meet back here on the ship's deck in 30 minutes. And may God be with us both."

Cautiously, Deveau and Second Mate John Wright moved across the deck of the silent ship. Timbers creaked and a few sails flapped in the wind. Otherwise, the *Mary Celeste* was quiet. Too quiet.

Deveau stealthily crept down the stairs into the ship's hold. The hundreds of barrels all looked intact. There was no sign of any crew even down here. Meanwhile, Wright, with many glances over his shoulder, carefully explored

the front of the ship. However, he found nothing unusual either. Deveau discovered the
moldy remains of a child's meal, but otherwise,
the food and supplies were all accounted for
and in good shape.

It wasn't long before the two men were
back on the deck. "Report," barked Deveau, fear
making his voice unnaturally harsh.

"There's no one here, sir," Wright said, his
eyes wide with fear. "And," he continued, staring out over the vast, empty ocean, "there's no
sign of where they've gone. They've just—well,
they've just vanished!"

READY TO CROSS THE ATLANTIC

On November 5, 1872, the *Mary Celeste* set sail from New York harbor. Loaded with 1,701 barrels full of high-strength alcohol (which is used to make wine stronger but can't be drunk on its own), the ship was bound for Genoa, Italy. At the helm was Captain Benjamin Spooner Briggs, a man with a reputation for being brave, fair to his crew, and well liked. He'd spent most of his life at sea, captained more than five ships, and owned many more.

The *Mary Celeste* was known as the *Amazon* when she was first launched in 1861. You can see the ship's original name on the flag on the top of the mast.

Mary Celeste

Captain Benjamin Spooner Briggs had captained many ships before he took command of the *Mary Celeste*. The year before the ship vanished, Briggs had thought about giving up the sea and buying a hardware store.

Briggs's crew of seven were extremely experienced and capable and could easily manage the large ship. The captain trusted them so much that he'd brought along his wife, Sarah, and their two-year-old daughter, Sophia. The captain had been delighted to discover that his old friend, Captain David Reed Morehouse, was also in New York with his wife. Briggs and Morehouse had known each other since they were young men and had served together as sailors.

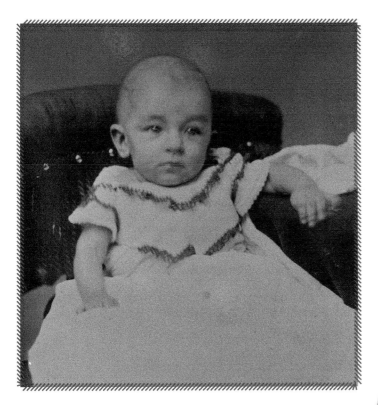

Sophia Briggs, Captain Briggs's daughter, had turned two just days before the *Mary Celeste* sailed from New York.

The captains and their wives had dinner together on November 4 and were pleased to learn that Morehouse's ship, the *Dei Gratia*, would soon also be bound for Italy. The two captains happily made plans to have dinner again in a few weeks on the other side of the Atlantic.

OMINOUS BEGINNINGS

The *Mary Celeste*'s voyage got off to a bad start. When the ship was just a short distance off shore, the weather turned so bad that the vessel was forced to stop and anchor for two days. Then on November 7, the winds became light and were blowing eastward, toward Europe. The *Mary Celeste* was finally able to resume her journey.

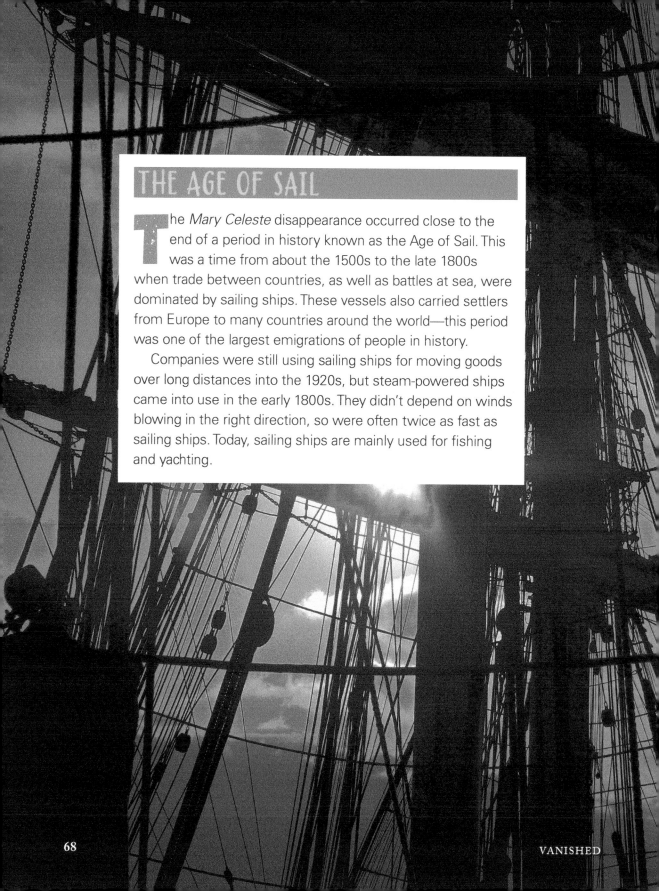

THE AGE OF SAIL

The *Mary Celeste* disappearance occurred close to the end of a period in history known as the Age of Sail. This was a time from about the 1500s to the late 1800s when trade between countries, as well as battles at sea, were dominated by sailing ships. These vessels also carried settlers from Europe to many countries around the world—this period was one of the largest emigrations of people in history.

Companies were still using sailing ships for moving goods over long distances into the 1920s, but steam-powered ships came into use in the early 1800s. They didn't depend on winds blowing in the right direction, so were often twice as fast as sailing ships. Today, sailing ships are mainly used for fishing and yachting.

David Reed Morehouse was captain of the *Dei Gratia*, the ship that found the abandoned *Mary Celeste*. He was from Nova Scotia, Canada, where both ships were built.

Captain Morehouse set sail from New York on November 15. On December 4, his ship, the *Dei Gratia*, was about 965 kilometers (600 miles) west of Portugal when he saw a strange sight. There in the distance was another ship. That wasn't so odd, since even in this desolate area of the North Atlantic there were many ships sailing between Europe and North America. But what *was* strange was that she seemed to be just drifting over the ocean waves. Some of her sails were down, while others were up, but torn.

NO ONE AT THE HELM

Morehouse watched the strange ship for some time through his spyglass, then called over his first mate.

"What do you make of this, Deveau?" asked the captain, pointing at the distant ship and handing the first mate the spyglass.

"I do not understand, sir," said Deveau after a few minutes of observing the vessel. "She's yawing, just drifting out of control."

"There must be something wrong," Morehouse said.

"But there's no distress signal flying," pointed out the first mate.

"I have not seen anyone steering her," the captain answered. "There's no one at the helm or on deck."

"Maybe that's just what they want us to think," said one of the crew who was standing nearby.

"Maybe that's what *who* wants us to think?" another asked.

"Pirates!" said the first crewman darkly. "This is what they do. They'll lure us on board, then take our ship the way they ambushed that one. It's a trap!"

"I've watched her long enough, men. There's no one on board," the captain said decisively. "Johnson, sail us closer to her. Wright, you continue to watch her deck for any sign of life. When we're near enough, Deveau, take two men with you and row over to investigate."

GONE, GONE, GONE

First Mate Deveau, along with John Wright (second mate) and John Johnson (helmsman, the person who steers a ship), headed over to the strangly drifting vessel. As they circled the ship to find a place to tie up,

Oliver Deveau, first mate of the *Dei Gratia*, thought the *Mary Celeste* would make him rich. Instead, it placed him under a cloud of suspicion.

they rowed by the stern (back) of the ship, where they saw her name: the *Mary Celeste*.

Deveau didn't want to take any chances so he left Johnson in the small boat to make sure it didn't drift away. With his pistol drawn, Deveau carefully eased himself over the ship's rail and stood motionless for a moment, listening intently. Wright was just behind him.

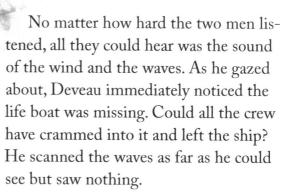

No matter how hard the two men listened, all they could hear was the sound of the wind and the waves. As he gazed about, Deveau immediately noticed the life boat was missing. Could all the crew have crammed into it and left the ship? He scanned the waves as far as he could see but saw nothing.

Deveau realized that two of the hatches were open. Then he saw that one of the ship's pumps had been taken apart. He knew the pumps ran down from the deck to the bilge (the deepest part of the ship) to remove any seawater that might leak in. To test how much water was in the bilge, a crew member put ash on a metal pole, called a sounding rod, and lowered it into the pump. Then he pulled the rod out to see how far up the rod the wet ash extended.

Usually, crews kept the sounding rod in the pump or stowed away nearby. But this rod had been out on the deck, as if dropped in a hurry. When Deveau sounded the pump, he estimated that the *Mary Celeste* had only taken on about 1.2 meters (4 feet) of water. Most ships take on water during a voyage and that

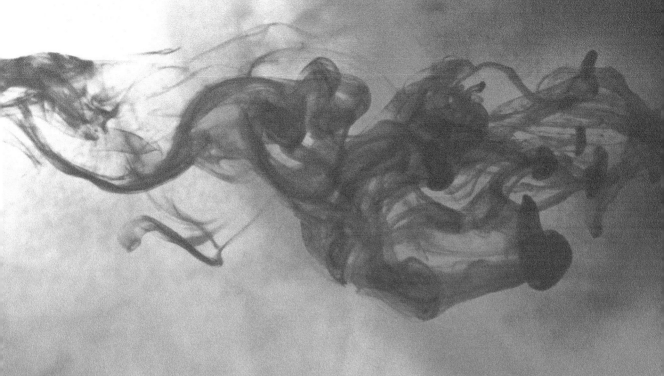

amount wasn't enough to make any experienced crew abandon ship. So where were they?

The rope used to hoist the main sail was also missing, to Deveau's surprise. Then he noticed a rope was tied tightly to the ship, with its other end trailing in the water and frayed. Could that be the missing mainsail rope? Why was it tied in the wrong place?

Wright examined the forecastle (the sailors' quarters at the front of the ship) while Deveau crept down into the main cabin. There, he was shocked to see the crew's smoking pipes. Sailors rarely went anywhere without their pipes. What had happened to make them leave even their pipes behind?

NO BLOOD, NO STRUGGLE

Deveau and Wright found that some of the cabins below deck were flooded and a pane of glass in a skylight was broken. As well, the ship's charts (maps of bodies of water) looked like they'd been tossed around. Navigational tools, such as the sextant (an instrument that uses the moon, stars, and sun to determine a ship's location in the ocean) and, later, the chronometer (a timepiece with a special mechanism for precisely finding a ship's position at sea), were found missing.

But the crew's clothes and other belongings were still in their cabins. If pirates had boarded the *Mary Celeste*, they would have taken anything of value they could get their hands on. That included the barrels of alcohol that were still neatly stowed in the ship's hold. Even Captain

The first practical chronometer wasn't invented until the late 1700s. This timepiece allowed a ship's navigator to determine the vessel's longitude (its east-west position) using the sun, moon, or stars.

Briggs's wife's harmonium (a keyboard instrument like an organ) was dry and in good condition. Deveau estimated there was still enough food and supplies on board to last six months.

Neither Deveau nor Wright could find any clue to what had happened to the crew or the captain's wife and daughter. There was no sign of a struggle—no overturned chairs or smashed walls, no blood spattered anywhere. The last entry in the ship's logbook (a sort of travel diary that records important information about a ship's progress, repairs, and condition) was from nine days earlier, recorded at 5:00 a.m. on November 25. It stated that the *Mary Celeste* was within reach of the Azores, a collection of nine islands about 1,370 kilometers (850 miles) west of Portugal. Even with the water in the hold, Deveau estimated the *Mary Celeste* could have sailed the distance easily.

So where were the crew? Why would an experienced sailor like Captain Briggs abandon a seaworthy ship? With a shiver, Deveau decided it was time to return to the *Dei Gratia.* But the cargo of barrels had given him an idea.

NEXT STOP: GIBRALTAR

Deveau reported his findings to Captain Morehouse, downplaying the curious things he and Wright had observed. He wanted to persuade the captain to put him and two crew members aboard the *Mary Celeste* and let them sail her to a harbor. Why? Because Deveau hoped that he and the whole crew of the *Dei Gratia* would be awarded the abandoned ship's salvage rights. This was a payment sailors received from a ship's

Gibraltar, where the *Mary Celeste* finally arrived on December 13, 1872. It's famous for the Rock of Gibraltar, seen here on the right.

owners for finding a drifting ship and bringing her to port. Deveau estimated each of the crew might receive more money in the salvage award than they earned in a year.

Morehouse knew that the ghost ship—what sailors back then called any ship found sailing without her crew—had been registered in Great Britain, so he decided the ship should go to the nearest British harbor, where the proper authorities could investigate the mystery of the vanished crew. The closest British port was Gibraltar, on a peninsula south of Spain, where the Atlantic Ocean meets the Mediterranean Sea, and only about 1,300 kilometers (800 miles)—a week's sail—away.

Morehouse knew how much the extra money from the salvage reward could mean to his men. So even though it would be tough sailing each of the

ships with just half a crew, he agreed to allow Deveau and sailors Augustus Anderson and Charles Lund to guide the *Mary Celeste* to Gibraltar. It took the three men two days to repair the ship's rigging (ropes and sails). Morehouse sailed the *Dei Gratia* to Gibraltar so he and his crew could report their findings about the ghost ship. They would also be close to the damaged *Mary Celeste* and could offer help if it was needed.

The *Dei Gratia* arrived in Gibraltar on December 12, 1872, while the *Mary Celeste* arrived the next day— Friday the 13th. Morehouse gasped when he laid eyes on his first mate. Deveau looked gaunt and exhausted. No wonder, when there had been just three of them to do work that normally took eight men. When the captain congratulated the first mate on reaching Gibraltar, Deveau wearily responded, "I don't know that I would attempt it again."

A JINXED SHIP?

Bad luck seemed to follow the *Mary Celeste*—originally called the *Amazon*—right from the beginning. Her first captain came down with pneumonia just days after taking command and died at the beginning of her initial voyage. He was only the first of three captains to die aboard the ship.

Under command of her second captain, the *Mary Celeste* hit a fishing boat. While in a shipyard for repairs, a fire broke out on board. She collided with another ship in the English Channel, then ran aground during a storm off Nova Scotia, Canada.

After the crew's mysterious disappearance, the *Mary Celeste* had 17 owners in just 13 years. "Of all the unlucky vessels I ever heard of," said one of the ghost ship's owners, "she was the most unlucky."

DASTARDLY DEEDS?

As Captain Morehouse had expected, an official investigation into the matter was held in Gibraltar to try to uncover what had happened aboard the *Mary Celeste* that led to the disappearance of her crew. To some investigators, it was all too clear what had occurred. They were certain Morehouse and the crew of the *Dei Gratia* had killed the crew of the *Mary Celeste* and thrown them overboard, then sailed the ship to Gibraltar to claim the salvage rights.

A PIRATE'S FAVORITE: THE BRIGANTINE

Both the *Mary Celeste* and the *Dei Gratia* were a type of ship known as a brigantine. These vessels have two masts to hold sails. The mast at the front (bow) of the ship is called the foremast and it held four or five rectangular sails (called square sails), each one hanging above a slightly larger sail. The other mast was farther back on the ship and was called the mainmast. It held a number of triangular sails, with one or two square sails at the top.

Because a brigantine was fast and easy to maneuver, it was a favorite of pirates. In fact, its name comes from the Italian word *brigantino,* which means "brigand "or "bandit."

But this dastardly theory had to be dismissed. Not only were the captains of the two ships friends, but there was no damage or blood on the deck, nor any other indications of fighting between the crews of the two ships. Soon many naval experts and journalists came up with lots of other theories to explain the mysterious disappearance of the crew of the *Mary Celeste.*

Some investigators said pirates must have killed the entire crew. But they conveniently ignored the lack of blood, no signs of any skirmishes on the ship, and the fact that nothing had been stolen.

A waterspout is a type of tornado that swirls over water. Most waterspouts are rotating columns of air, but they don't usually suck up water.

SEAQUAKES AND WATERSPOUTS

Another explanation was that a waterspout, a funnel-shaped cloud heavy with rain and spray, had swept everyone off the ship. Or perhaps the *Mary Celeste* had been hit by a hurricane, a violent storm with high winds and driving rain or hail.

The crew of the ship could have been swept off the deck by a seaquake, turbulence caused by an eruption deep below the ocean's surface. Seaquakes can cause tsunamis, huge waves that overturn ships and cause extensive damage along coastlines. Another type of unusually large and deadly wave is the "rogue wave," caused by high winds and strong currents, and striking far out at sea.

FAR-FETCHED THEORIES

Because there was so little factual information, people came up with all kinds of strange theories for what had happened to the *Mary Celeste*. For instance, when the *Mary Celeste*'s cargo was unloaded in Gibraltar, authorities were surprised to discover that 9 of the 1,701 barrels of alcohol were empty, even though they were undamaged. Who—or what—had emptied the barrels?

One theory was that the ship's crew members got drunk on the alcohol in the cargo, murdered Briggs and his family, then escaped in the lifeboat. But investigators had to eliminate this solution. For one thing, Captain Briggs was strongly opposed to drinking, so he wouldn't have allowed his crew to drink any of the alcohol. But more important, the liquid in the barrels was commercial alcohol, which is not for drinking straight. The men would likely have become very sick before they became drunk; it would have been impossible for them to carry out any kind of plan while they were that sick.

And then in 1913, an article in England's *Strand Magazine* reported that the captain had challenged one of his crew to a swimming race. The rest of the crew and the captain's family watched from a platform while the two men swam around the ship. However, disaster struck, the expert explained, when sharks ate the swimmers and the platform collapsed, dumping everyone else into the sea. Since no trace of a platform was found on the ship, not much attention was paid to this far-fetched explanation.

READ ALL ABOUT IT

Many stories were told about the mysterious events on the *Mary Celeste*, and the tales became more incredible each time they were recounted. One of the reasons there are so many myths and so much incorrect information about the ship is because of the tale "J. Habakuk Jephson's Statement."

This short story was published by Sir Arthur Conan Doyle. Today, most people know him as the creator of the brilliant detective Sherlock Holmes, but in 1884, he was a young writer just trying to get his work published.

In Doyle's story, the legendary ship is called the *Marie Celeste*, and many people still assume that's its correct name. Although Doyle used many facts from the actual disappearance, he introduced fictional details, such as that none of the lifeboats were missing and that the ship was in almost perfect condition when discovered.

THE CLUE IN THE BARRELS

Investigators examined the barrels more carefully. They found that all of the barrels were made of oak. But the nine empty barrels were constructed out of red oak, not white oak like all the others. That might sound like a small difference, but it was important—and possibly deadly.

Red oak is a much more porous wood than white oak and was usually used only for shipping dry goods. The alcohol leaking out of the red oak barrels would have evaporated quickly, but the smell and vapor would have built up in the hold (the ship's cargo space). The crew would have known that as the barrels rubbed together while the ship was buffeted by the waves, the steel bands on the barrels could grate against each other and cause sparks. If the sparks mixed with the alcohol fumes ... Were they just minutes away from a deadly explosion?

"HEAVY WEATHER" ON THE NORTH ATLANTIC

What made this voyage so different from any of Captain Briggs's previous trips was that he had never carried a cargo as dangerous as commercial alcohol before. The liquor made him very nervous. It's possible he became concerned about a buildup of fumes in the hold.

After all, the *Mary Celeste*'s log showed that the ship had battled what sailors call "heavy weather" for two weeks. During November 1872, ships in the North Atlantic Ocean experienced the worst weather since record keeping began. Strong winds, high waves, and driving rain meant that hundreds of vessels were lost or abandoned when they capsized or took on too much water, and many experienced sailors died.

During the heavy weather, the hatch on the hold containing all the barrels of alcohol had to be securely latched. On the morning of November 25, when there was calm weather for the first time in days, the captain may have opened the hold to disperse any fumes. If the vapors poured out suddenly, Briggs might have become afraid that the alcohol was about to explode. Perhaps he even heard an ominous rumbling.

One of the bilge pumps on the ship was found to be full of scraps. The crew might have overestimated how much water was in the bilge and feared that the ship was sinking.

Another reason they may have left the ship was because Briggs didn't see the coast of Europe when he expected to. That could have led him to think there was a problem with the ship's chronometer. Briggs wouldn't have been sure exactly where he was or how near or far from land. He may have felt it necessary to act quickly to save the lives of his crew and family.

In the late 1800s, ships had no radios or other electronic communication systems. Briggs's only way to send out a distress message was to use the ship's signal flags—but if no ships were close enough to read the message, the flags were useless. Briggs and his crew must have scanned the horizon desperately, hoping some ship would see their emergency flags and rescue them.

Experts at the time of the trial speculated that Briggs ordered everyone into the lifeboat, telling them it was just for a short time, so there was no need to take any food or belongings with them. The captain's unfamiliarity with alcohol as cargo likely pushed him to the extreme measure of abandoning the ship.

Artists imagined how the captain's family and the crew of the *Mary Celeste* must have felt crammed into a lifeboat, as the ship sailed farther and farther away from them.

DRIFTING IN THE MIDDLE OF THE OCEAN

Although the crew would have attached the boat to the *Mary Celeste* with a strong rope, they may have failed to secure it properly in their hurry. If the wind picked up and blew the ship and the little lifeboat apart, the rope would have frayed and eventually snapped. With all its sails still up, the *Mary Celeste* would soon have blown far away from the lifeboat.

Briggs's family and crew would have watched in despair as the *Mary Celeste* disappeared over the horizon. There was no food or water on the little lifeboat. They knew they faced death by hunger, thirst, or drowning. It was unlikely another boat would reach them in time. Unlike modern lifeboats, theirs had no flares or radio—no way of signaling for help. The lifeboat was barely big enough for the nine adults.

Soon after the last entry in the ship's log, the weather took another turn for the worse. Days away from the nearest land and surrounded by nothing but deep ocean, they hoped another ship would sail by and rescue them. But as time passed, that possibility became more and more unlikely. They had no fresh water to drink, the sun beat down during the day, and the temperatures plummeted when night fell. It was almost impossible for the little boat to stay afloat in the high winds and driving waves.

GUILTY OR INNOCENT?

The inquiry in Gibraltar lasted three months. In the end, the British judge praised Captain Morehouse and his crew for their great courage. Not only had they taken the risk of dividing the crew and sailing both the *Dei Gratia* and the *Mary Celeste* with only half a crew each, but they had shown great skill in successfully bringing both ships safely to Gibraltar.

However, it was obvious that with no definite solution to the mystery, the *Dei Gratia* crewmen were still under suspicion. Although the court found no evidence of foul play, the crew received only a fraction of the money they were entitled to in salvage rights.

It was clear the authorities were not totally convinced of the sailors' innocence.

No trace was ever found of any of the *Mary Celeste*'s crew members or of any of the missing equipment. If the crew had mutinied, killed the captain and his family, and made it to land in the lifeboat, it's unlikely that all of them could have kept their dreadful secret. And if the *Dei Gratia*'s crew were behind the disappearance, it's certain someone would have eventually told the real story. But no drunken admittance of guilt or deathbed confession was ever reported. It's as if the crew and passengers evaporated, just like the nine barrels of alcohol.

THE LEGEND LIVES ON

The *Mary Celeste* sailed the seas again after the curious incident of 1872, but only for about another 13 years. By then, she was in poor condition. Her last owner tried to commit insurance fraud by over-insuring the cargo. That means he paid insurance for more than the cargo was worth. Then he deliberately wrecked the ship in a bay somewhere off Haiti and tried to get the money back from the insurance company. The *Mary Celeste* slipped below the waves, out of sight. Her legend lived on, but the actual ship was mostly forgotten.

In 2001, an expedition used a magnetometer (which detects iron or magnetic metals) to examine a wreck in the Haitian bay where the *Mary Celeste* sank many years before. The scientists confirmed that no other vessel had been wrecked here, so they were sure they'd found the last resting place of the legendary ship. Careful analysis of wood samples from the wreck revealed that it had been built in New England or Canada's Maritimes. Since the *Mary Celeste* was built in Nova Scotia, this was another confirming detail.

But that's likely the only mystery about the *Mary Celeste* that will ever be solved. Although the Age of Sail is long past (see page 68), the oceans still keep many deep secrets and people continue to wonder about the fate of the crew and passengers of this legendary ship.

THE VAST OCEANS DEEP

It may seem incredible that the crew and passengers of the *Mary Celeste* could vanish without a trace. But in March 2014, the world discovered that an entire plane with 239 people on board could also disappear. Malaysia Airlines flight 370 was flying from Kuala Lumpur, Malaysia, to Beijing, China, when it vanished in the Pacific Ocean west of Australia.

Searchers combed the ocean using satellite imagery, sonar technology, echo sounders, and video cameras, as well as underwater robots. Despite the location technology standard on all planes today, the strong winds, high waves, and deep ocean waters made the beacons, known as pingers, impossible to find. The flight recorder, or black box (which is actually usually orange), was also never found. The search for the plane is the largest and most expensive in aviation history and is still continuing.

SEARCHING UNDERWATER

Today, it would be easier to solve a mystery like the fate of the *Mary Celeste*. Like planes and cars, modern ships are equipped with a data recorder, more commonly known as a "black box."

In ships, the black box is called a voyage data recorder (VDR). It collects data from the many sensors on board the vessel. Using the Global Positioning System (GPS), the VDR records the date, time, and position of the ship, as well as its speed and the direction in which it's traveling. But the VDR can also collect information such as how deep the water is below the ship (thanks to information from an echo sounder), whether fire doors are closed, and how the engine is functioning.

The VDR digitizes, compresses, and stores all this information in a tamper-proof unit. This protective storage unit can withstand the shock of an extreme impact, as well as high pressure or the heat of an explosion or fire. Some VDRs are fixed in place, while others can float so they're easy to retrieve if a ship sinks.

A voyage data recorder on a ship's deck.

Modern forensic chemistry would have helped scientists investigating the mystery of the *Mary Celeste*. This branch of law enforcement involves analyzing chemical changes to help reconstruct what happened in an accident or crime.

Forensic chemists use many techniques, including gas chromatography, a process for determining what's in a gas by separating its components. Analyzing the air in the hold on the *Mary Celeste* might have given investigators important information for solving the mystery. Another way to analyze chemicals is with infrared radiation. The machine chemists use for this is called a spectrophotometer.

Luminol is a chemical that reacts with particles in blood, making it easy to detect blood (even if it's been partially cleaned up) at crime scenes. Ultraviolet light can also reveal the presence of chemicals and other body fluids not ordinarily visible. Forensic chemists look at how substances react to various chemicals and use what's known as microchemistry to identify the chemical composition of tiny particles, such as fragments left after bombs are exploded or guns are fired.

To make sure they don't contaminate a crime scene while investigating it, forensic researchers wear clean room suits, also known as bunny suits.

AMBER ROOM

RUSSIA'S MISSING TREASURE

LENINGRAD, RUSSIA, 1941

"Bystro! Bystro!" Quickly! Quickly!

Anatoly Kuchumov ran frantically across the floor of the Amber Room, yelling at his staff. As the curator (the person in charge of a museum or special collection) at Russia's Catherine Palace museum, he was proud of all the treasures in the museum's collection, but this hall was his favorite.

"Hold that padding in place on the wall," Kuchumov shouted, pointing at a woman with her arms full of cotton stuffing. "Fasten the burlap over it. Nothing must show through it, nothing! Do you hear me?"

With his staff's help, Kuchumov had packed up paintings, lamps, and other treasures to send them away and protect them from the approaching Nazis. But he was forced to leave the Amber Room behind. All that he and his staff could do was try to hide the shimmering, golden room. And it was breaking his heart.

Layers of fabric enveloped the chamber's radiant glow, transforming the hall into a shabby, dim space. Would it be enough to fool the advancing soldiers?

"Boris, spread sand on the floor—it will protect the wood and may even hide it a little. *Bystro! Bystro!* Now, all of you, get out while you can," ordered the curator. "Go home and prepare for the invasion."

Kuchumov looked around the Amber Room one last time, patting the wall lovingly. "*Do svidaniya*," he whispered sadly. Until we meet again.

Then he turned and hurried out into the night.

A ROOM FIT FOR A KING

For more than 300 years, the world has been amazed by stories of the glorious Amber Room. Over 100,000 slivers of amber in many different shapes and colors were fitted together like a priceless jigsaw puzzle of images, swirls, and intricate patterns. The perfectly shaped transparent slices of amber were backed with gold foil. When the 500 candles that illuminated the room were lit, the yellow, brown, and honey tones flickered and gleamed.

But the walls were decorated with more than the mosaic patterns of medallions, scallops, and garlands of amber. Scenes such as chariot battles, sailing ships, and castles had also been meticulously engraved backward on the inside of tiny fragments of amber. These were then assembled and polished until they were transparent.

A corner of the incredible Amber Room.

MORE PRECIOUS THAN GOLD

In 1701, when the idea of the Amber Room first took shape, amber was 12 times as valuable as gold. The room was originally built as a study for King Friedrich I of Prussia (a country that today is part of Germany). Craftsmen worked with many tons of amber, gold, and mirrors to create this incredible chamber.

Panels in the Amber Room were made up of pieces of amber carefully fitted together. They form images and patterns, as shown in this photo of the recreated room (see page 117).

But before it was completed, Friedrich I died, in 1713. His heir, Friedrich Wilhelm I, had no interest in the Amber Room. However, he knew that Russian czar Peter the Great had been captivated by it. The Prussian king wanted the czar to join him in an alliance against Sweden. So Friedrich Wilhelm swapped the room he didn't want for the military help he needed.

The Amber Room was taken apart, loaded onto 18 horse-drawn wagons, and delivered to St. Petersburg, Russia. But battles with various European countries kept Czar Peter busy and the panels remained in their crates.

After Peter died in 1725, his daughter, Elizabeth, eventually became the ruler and she had the Amber Room reassembled. The panels were installed in the Winter Palace (today home to Russia's famous Hermitage Museum).

But the new location was bigger than the original room. So mirrors were added, as well as sections painted to look like amber. Then Elizabeth decided the Amber Room would look better in her summer residence, the Catherine Palace. So in 1755, workmen carefully carried the panels by hand to their new home. This new room was even bigger than the last, so more mirrors and painted panels were added.

THE INCREDIBLE STONE THAT ISN'T

Although many people consider amber a gemstone, it's actually the remains of prehistoric tree resin. If you've ever seen thick, sticky liquid oozing down the bark of a pine tree, then you've seen the beginning of amber. The amber used to create the Amber Room was found around the Baltic Sea in what are now the European countries of Lithuania, Poland, and Russia.

More than 30 million years ago, logs and branches of resinous trees washed down to the sea. Before the resin dried, the wood was buried under wet clay and sand and hardened into what we call amber. Eventually, pieces popped up to the surface and washed ashore.

A scorpion embedded in amber.

Amber can be burned, releasing an exotic aroma. In German, amber is called *Bernstein,* or "burn stone." When it's rubbed with wool, amber develops a static charge. The Greek word for amber is *elektron,* which is the origin of the word "electricity."

THE EIGHTH WONDER OF THE WORLD

Shortly after Catherine the Great became czarina of Russia in 1762, she ordered that the painted sections be replaced with real amber. Craftsmen also carved decorative amber panels for over the doors, built amber-covered columns out from the walls, and altogether added another 450 kilograms (990 pounds) of amber to the room.

The four middle panels of the room showed Italian-style scenes of the five senses (the senses of touch and smell were combined). Even some of the furniture was decorated with amber, including mirror frames, chests of drawers, and tables. The floors weren't amber, but they were intricately inlaid with 15 types of wood to create beautiful swirling patterns.

The Catherine Palace became the Amber Room's home in 1755. Russia's czars lived here in the summer.

Elaborate golden gates guard the Catherine Palace.

By the time the Amber Room was finally finished in 1770, it was 17 meters (56 feet) long, big enough for a large school bus to park inside with lots of room left over. A total of 5,440 kilograms (6 tons) of amber had gone into its creation, and the room was worth more than $142 million in today's dollars.

Over the next 150 years, royals and nobles from all over Europe flocked to see the incredible glowing Amber Room. Russians claimed it was the eighth wonder of the world. After the Russian Revolution in 1917 and the abolishment of the Russian royal family, Catherine Palace became a museum. Now, common people of the new Soviet Union could gaze at the stunning artwork in the stately home. The Amber Room became the most popular exhibit in the entire city of St. Petersburg, which had been renamed Leningrad.

But there were even greater changes coming for the Amber Room.

DINOSAURS IN AMBER?

The Jurassic Park movies are based on the idea of scientists creating dinosaurs from ancient DNA. The experts cloned the huge beasts from genetic material found in mosquitoes trapped for millions of years in amber. The semi-precious stone that lines the walls of the Amber Room may also hold insects that are supposedly full of dinosaur blood containing the animals' DNA.

However, scientists have been unable to detect any ancient DNA in insects that have been trapped in amber as old as 60,000 years. In samples older than this, the odds of being able to extract DNA are even slimmer. Since dinosaurs disappeared from the earth about 65 million years ago, you don't need to worry about encountering a stegosaurus in the street.

OPERATION BARBAROSSA

On September 1, 1939, Germany invaded Poland, starting World War II. In December 1940, Adolf Hitler, head of Germany and leader of the Nazi forces, decided to attack the Soviet Union as well, in the offensive code-named Operation Barbarossa.

The German invasion of the Soviet Union was the largest attack in the history of war, and preparations took about a year and a half. Operation Barbarossa, which was named after a fearless German leader from the 1100s, involved 4 million German soldiers, 600,000 tanks and trucks, and 625,000 horses.

After all the preparations, on June 22, 1941, the Nazis launched the offensive, winning victory after victory. The Soviet soldiers pushed back, but they were no match for the well-trained, well-equipped German soldiers. Russian war experts estimated the Germans would be in Leningrad and its beautiful museums in just weeks.

News of the invasion filled Anatoly Kuchumov with dread. He knew Hitler encouraged his soldiers to grab any valuables and treasures they found and send them back to Germany. The Nazi leader dreamed of building the world's best museum and making it the center of art for Europe and beyond.

During the Siege of Leningrad, many people died of starvation, especially during the winter of 1941–42.

Kuchumov and his staff immediately began crating up the treasures in the Catherine Palace and other museums. They had no idea how soon the Germans would strike their city and its beautiful museum, so they worked tirelessly. Soon they ran out of crates and paper, so instead they protected priceless artwork with grass and hay. The workers even used gowns that had belonged to past czarinas to wrap the treasures as the staff packed them into trunks.

Some of the museum's vases were too large and heavy to move. Staff filled them with water to absorb the shock of any bombing and keep the valuable urns from smashing. Meanwhile, other staff members and archivists took photos of the rooms and made notes. They hoped that one day the treasures would

The staff at the Catherine Palace worked for days desperately packing paintings, statues, and other treasures into crates. Some workers developed nosebleeds from leaning over the packing crates for so long.

be returned and could be put back exactly where they belonged.

But one very important treasure in the Catherine Palace had not been packed.

HIDING IN PLAIN SIGHT

Kuchumov was certain Hitler would especially want the Amber Room, not only because it was so valuable but also because it had been German originally. That made the chamber especially important to the Nazi leader. So Kuchumov and his staff tried to remove the treasured amber panels from the palace walls. But the heating in the museum had dried out the amber and made it brittle. No matter how carefully the Catherine Palace staff tried to remove the panels, they found to their horror that the amber crumbled. It couldn't be moved.

What would they do now? How could they protect this glorious room with the Nazis coming closer and closer? Kuchumov decided the only thing to do was to disguise the amber panels and hope to deceive the Nazis.

The curator ordered his staff to first cover the room completely in gauze and cotton wadding to protect the amber. They topped this with rough burlap. The windows were crisscrossed with tape, then boarded up to protect them and make it difficult to see anything in the room.

Kuchumov and his staff hoped the Germans would quickly pass through the room thinking it was completely unimportant. The workers also spread sand on the beautifully crafted floor to protect it from soldiers' heavy boots. Kuchumov wondered if it would be enough to save the Amber Room.

Eight days after the Germans invaded the Soviet Union, 17 train cars full of priceless paintings, sculptures, and jewels steamed out of Leningrad, bound for Siberia. There, the treasures would be protected, hidden far from the advancing Nazis. Kuchumov was ordered to accompany the crates. He wrote in his diary: "When will we ever come home and what will be our future and what of those we leave behind?" Beyond a doubt, he was thinking about the Amber Room.

By the end of August, Germans had taken control of a key railway terminal just outside Leningrad and cut off the city from the rest of the world. It was too late to get out any more treasures. On September 17, the Nazis took over Leningrad and overran its museums.

NAZIS INVADE THE PALACE!

The German soldiers pounded up the marble staircase of the Catherine Palace and bashed down the doors. Some of the soldiers flung themselves, exhausted, on the furniture, carelessly propping up their muddy boots on the precious chairs and settees. But one private decided to explore his new barracks. His sergeant had filled the soldiers' heads with tales of priceless Soviet treasure in the imperial palaces, and the private wanted to see it.

The Nazis had advanced into Leningrad so quickly that the private figured the Russians hadn't had time to hide any of their valuables. If he could find that Amber Room the sergeant had told them about, maybe there'd be a promotion for him. Perhaps he could even steal a very special souvenir for himself! So while other soldiers settled into their palace home, the young soldier raced from room to room.

But all the Nazi soldier could find were empty rooms. In fact, one of them was so dilapidated there was even sand on the ground. It made him furious! Where was all the treasure they'd been promised? Where was that room made of *Bernstein* (amber) the sergeant had told them about?

Frustrated, the private kicked at the doorway until he knocked a gaping hole in it. That made him feel a little better, so he looked around for something else to wreck. He whipped out his knife and dug it into the fabric wall. He ripped at the burlap and tore viciously at the padding behind it. And then he gasped!

This was the official flag of the Soviet Union during World War II. The hammer represents workers and the sickle stands for the country's peasants. The star is for the rule of the Communist Party.

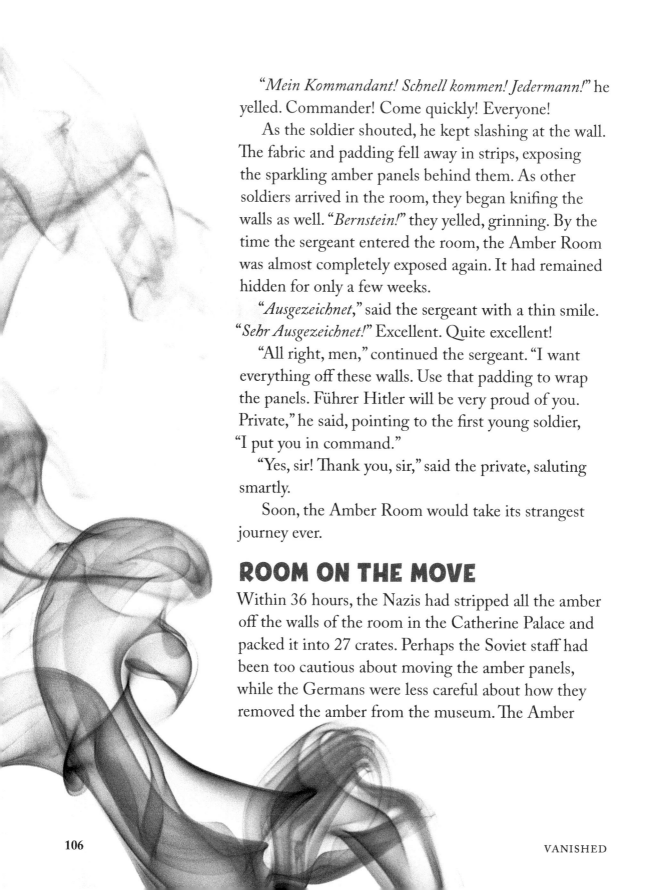

"*Mein Kommandant! Schnell kommen! Jedermann!*" he yelled. Commander! Come quickly! Everyone!

As the soldier shouted, he kept slashing at the wall. The fabric and padding fell away in strips, exposing the sparkling amber panels behind them. As other soldiers arrived in the room, they began knifing the walls as well. "*Bernstein!*" they yelled, grinning. By the time the sergeant entered the room, the Amber Room was almost completely exposed again. It had remained hidden for only a few weeks.

"*Ausgezeichnet,*" said the sergeant with a thin smile. "*Sehr Ausgezeichnet!*" Excellent. Quite excellent!

"All right, men," continued the sergeant. "I want everything off these walls. Use that padding to wrap the panels. Führer Hitler will be very proud of you. Private," he said, pointing to the first young soldier, "I put you in command."

"Yes, sir! Thank you, sir," said the private, saluting smartly.

Soon, the Amber Room would take its strangest journey ever.

ROOM ON THE MOVE

Within 36 hours, the Nazis had stripped all the amber off the walls of the room in the Catherine Palace and packed it into 27 crates. Perhaps the Soviet staff had been too cautious about moving the amber panels, while the Germans were less careful about how they removed the amber from the museum. The Amber

Königsberg Castle, where the Amber Room panels arrived in October 1941.

Room was on its way to the museum in Königsberg Castle, in the German town of Königsberg, just over the border from Russia. There, the amber panels were put on display so the Nazis could enjoy their stolen treasure.

Königsberg is on the coast of the Baltic Sea, where much of the amber from the famous room had originated more than 200 years earlier. The unusual material was especially appreciated there. The castle museum's director, Alfred Rohde, loved amber. It mesmerized him and he spent hours staring at it on the walls of his museum.

In April 1945, American troops found stolen artwork and other German loot in this church in Germany.

However, he couldn't enjoy it for long. By late 1943, the war was going badly for the Nazis. Germany's enemies, the Allies (including Canada, France, Great Britain, the Soviet Union, and the United States), were threatening Königsberg. Rohde had to take the Amber Room apart, and it was crated up yet again. In August 1944, bombing raids destroyed the city and reduced the castle to rubble.

Soviet troops took over the city in April 1945. The first thing they did was search the area around the destroyed castle for the Amber Room. But there was no trace of it. The dungeons below the castle where some witnesses swore the glowing panels had been stored were empty.

The Amber Room had disappeared.

HIDDEN IN THE THEATER

It's hard to believe, but sometimes vanishing is the best way artwork can be saved.

In the early 1900s, vaudeville was popular in theaters. These shows involved singers, jugglers, and comedians who traveled across North America. Each theater where they performed provided scenery and backdrops. Week after week, the backdrops were repainted to suit each new vaudeville troupe. Eventually, the backdrops fell apart from overuse.

The Winter Garden Theatre in Toronto, Canada, was a famous vaudeville theater. But then this style of theater went out of favor, and in 1928, the Winter Garden closed. No one reentered the theater until the 1980s.

When they did, they were shocked to discover the vaudeville backdrops, forgotten in the Winter Garden's darkness. Today, they're the world's largest collection of vaudeville scenery, and you can see some of them when you visit the theater.

WHO OWNS IT?

After World War II ended in Europe on May 8, 1945, a group called the Monuments, Fine Arts and Archives (MFAA) Section unit of the United States Army was given the task of finding art stolen by the Nazis. Once the MFAA found stolen artwork, it had to figure out who owned it. That proved to be difficult, since bombs, fires, and looters had destroyed evidence of ownership, such as bank records and insurance policies. Today, computers help historians search thousands of websites in minutes to check documents, but that technology wasn't yet available.

As World War II was ending in 1945, American soldiers found this painting and others hidden in a German salt mine.

For six years, about 60 MFAA researchers searched Europe for stolen artwork. Art experts with the United States National Archives estimate about 20 percent of all the art in Europe was seized by the Nazis.

More than 100,000 works of art have never been returned to their owners, according to a stolen art register. As with the Amber Room, art historians and descendants of the families who originally owned them still wonder where they are.

Allied troops found gold, paintings, and other treasures stored deep in a salt mine in Germany.

ONLY QUESTIONS, NO ANSWERS

After World War II ended and there wasn't a trace left of the Amber Room, art historians and Russian investigators began to speculate about where it could be. Maybe soldiers had broken it up and sold it off in pieces. But people disagree on whether it was the German, Russian, or Allied soldiers who divided up the amber panels and whether they sold the pieces to civilians or to other soldiers. If this were true, surely some of these pieces would have surfaced by now.

WORLD WAR II ENDS

Hitler committed suicide on April 30, 1945, and World War II ended in Europe on May 8 when Germany surrendered. Although Operation Barbarossa had been very successful at first for the Germans, this push for Russian land and treasure was the Nazis' undoing. They didn't have enough soldiers to wage war in massive Russia as well as in France, North Africa, Poland, let alone any other places.

The Siege of Leningrad lasted almost 900 days and finally ended on January 27, 1944. It was one of the longest and most destructive sieges in world history. More than 1 million people in Leningrad died, mostly from starvation. As the Nazis left Leningrad, they burned the Catherine Palace. When Anatoly Kuchumov was finally able to return, he must have wept when he saw the destruction, gasping at the sight of the empty walls where the Amber Room had once stood.

VANISHED

Eyewitnesses claim to have seen the famous room being loaded in crates onto a German submarine as the war was ending. The submarine was said to have just enough fuel to reach a certain location, where it then purposefully sank. The sub is still waiting deep below the water's surface, but its destination is long forgotten.

Some Russian historians believe the Germans tried to sneak the Amber Room out of the country on a ship but that it was torpedoed and sank to the bottom of the Baltic Sea.

The Nazi soldiers left the Amber Room and the entire Catherine Palace in ruins when they abandoned Leningrad.

A resident living on the shores of Lake Toplitz in Austria said that in April 1945 (just before the end of World War II), he saw 27 crates being dumped into the lake's deep waters. That's exactly the number of crates that the Amber Room was packed into when it was taken from Russia by the Germans. So in 2006, a group of American divers searched the bottom of Lake Toplitz for the fantastic chamber. They spent millions of dollars and used unmanned submarines and other high-tech search technology but found no trace of the Amber Room.

Some World War II researchers believe the Amber Room may be lost in the maze of underground tunnels and bunkers far below the streets of Königsberg. Or the panels may be waiting in unmarked crates in a forgotten storeroom or museum warehouse.

Treasure-hunting teams from many European countries, including Germany and Lithuania, think German soldiers managed to remove the Amber Room from Königsberg Castle. These groups believe it's hidden in a lagoon, a salt mine, or a silver mine. If that's the case, the fragile mosaics have likely completely fallen to pieces by now due to the dampness.

In 2004, a team of British investigative journalists concluded that the Amber Room no longer exists. They knew that when Königsberg was bombed in 1944, the castle had burned. The researchers found documents in the Russian National Archives stating that the Amber Room was still in the castle at the time and it also burned. Although amber looks like a gem, it can be destroyed through burning, since it is actually tree resin. The only problem with this theory is that so much amber would have burned with an overpowering sweet scent and no one remembers smelling such an incredible odor.

In 1946, the town of Königsberg became part of Russia (and was renamed Kaliningrad). The stone ruins of the castle were blown up by the Soviet government in 1968 and the site was turned into a city square. Since 2001, a German magazine has been sponsoring investigations into what remains of the castle's cellar. Thousands of items have been recovered, although there is still no trace of the Amber Room.

THE CURSE OF THE AMBER ROOM?

Stories have been told that connect the Amber Room with mysterious deaths. Alfred Rohde, the director of the Königsberg Castle museum, died of typhus (a disease causing high fever) while Russian police were investigating the room's disappearance. A top Russian intelligence officer died in a strange car crash after he talked to a writer about the Amber Room.

An investigator who said he'd discovered a radio message describing the fate of the room was found dead shortly after. One of the most famous Amber Room hunters was found dead in a forest.

The restored Amber Room in the Catherine Palace, sparkling and gleaming with a golden glow.

VISIT THE NEW AMBER ROOM!

Will the Amber Room mystery ever be forgotten? Not likely. After the war, the Catherine Palace was rebuilt, the artwork was brought back from Siberia, and the museum opened again. But it was still missing its most important showpiece: the Amber Room. So in 1979, Soviet craftsmen began working to recreate the glowing chamber in the Catherine Palace. They worked from photographs, written descriptions, and a few pieces hidden before the Nazis invaded.

The techniques the workers used dated back to the 1700s and had to be painstakingly relearned. Artisans recreated old dyes and glues, as well as long-forgotten techniques of carving, casting, and gilding. It cost $11 million. When a lack of funds threatened to end the project, a German gas company donated $3.5 million to the project as a goodwill gesture from Germany to Russia.

Construction was well underway when, in 1997, German police arrested a man for trying to sell a bejeweled mosaic. Art experts were amazed to identify the piece as the "touch and smell" panel from the Amber Room's mosaics of the five senses. The man was the son of a Nazi who had been one of the officers accompanying the Amber Room from Leningrad to Königsberg. Unfortunately, the officer had died years before and the son had no idea where his father had obtained the panel. The trail of the Amber Room had gone cold yet again.

On May 31, 2003, the new Amber Room was unveiled with great ceremony before a gathering of top

Restoring the Amber Room required years of hard work by many skilled artists and scientists.

world leaders. Russian president Vladimir Putin even made sure the sun would shine for this special event. Russian air force jets released freezing agents into the clouds over the city to prevent any rain—for the mere cost of about $1 million! The rebuilt Amber Room continues to dazzle art lovers and tourists from around the world, while text panels in the room remind visitors of the story of the original lost masterpiece.

WAITING IN THE DARKNESS?

Unfortunately, the most likely solution to the mystery of the Amber Room is that it was destroyed in Königsberg Castle in August 1944, either deliberately by the Nazis before they left the city or accidentally by the Allies as they bombed the castle. But that doesn't stop modern-day treasure hunters from dreaming of an incredible find. For Russians, the Amber Room represents the many people and things they lost during World War II, so it's much more than a chamber in a museum.

It seems that almost every year, another treasure hunter announces he knows the location of the Amber Room and is about to unveil it to the world. For instance, in 2008, a group claimed to have located a stash of Nazi gold and other treasure, including possibly the Amber Room, in underground storage rooms near Germany's border with the Czech Republic. But something always seems to happen just before the discovery is made and the investigator slips away into obscurity.

Perhaps the reason any claims about the Amber Room get so much publicity is because no one wants to believe that such a large, beautiful, and incredible treasure has really and truly completely vanished. Instead, people would like to think the Amber Room is still hidden away in an obscure cave or warehouse. If only someone can decipher the clues, then the original Amber Room will once more glow and astonish.

MAPPING AND TRACKING

Not all the artwork that the Nazis looted during World War II vanished forever. Thousands of paintings, sculptures, and statues were found and returned to their owners. But how were they found, and by whom?

The job of finding the stolen art was assigned to the Monuments, Fine Arts and Archives (MFAA) Section unit of the United States Army. About 350 architects, archivists, art curators, and librarians—men and women—from 13 countries hunted for more than 1,000 caches of art. They were searching for as many as 5 million pieces. The group used tips from civilians, overheard conversations, and deductive reasoning to uncover artwork hidden in castles, country estates, and jails. Some was even buried deep in mines.

The MFAA also used archaeological techniques to locate the artwork. Archaeology is the study of ancient peoples and their artifacts (tools, dishes, weapons, buttons and clasps from clothing, jewelry). Because it's easier to see changes in the patterns of trees, sand, fields, or rock formations from the sky, archaeologists often survey forests, jungles, and deserts from planes and helicopters. They take photos that may help identify possible historical sites that they will later travel to and explore.

During the war, the MFAA tried to save artwork and monuments using aerial photography. Allied air force troops were given images of historically and artistically important sites so they could try to avoid dropping bombs on these places.

Today, drones (remote-controlled unmanned aircraft) are also used for aerial photography. Archaeologists interpret the photos and decide where artwork or other treasures may be hidden or buried.

Satellite imagery is another current option for viewing an area to decide whether it's worth studying further. From high above the earth, orbiting satellites collect images of the planet.

Another technique for archaeological imaging is geophysical survey: using data-processing computer programs to make maps of archaeological features that lie buried below the earth's surface. The maps allow researchers to more easily visualize patterns and recognize irregularities.

Modern archaeologists can use GIS (Geographic Information System) technology to capture, analyze, and store the geographic data they collect. GIS allows researchers to create maps and models to help in their searches.

Today, drones make it easy for researchers to shoot aerial photos and videos.

Aerial photography lets scientists examine large areas of both cities and countryside.

ALCATRAZ PRISON BREAKOUT

CONVICTS' VANISHING ACT

Three men crouched low by the water's edge, struggling into their life jackets.

"Okay," whispered Frank Morris. "The raft's all blown up and ready to go. Pull your life jackets on, grab your paddles, and let's get outta here."

"Geez, that water's cold," said John Anglin, shivering in the cool night wind.

"Well, if you want to head back to your nice cozy prison cell, you be my guest," snarled Morris. "Just don't you go squealin' on us, not if you know what's good for you."

"Now, Frank, he didn't mean nothin'," said Clarence, John's brother.

"You two always stick up for each other. Why don't you just shut up and get that raft into the water," said Morris. "It's time for us to make tracks."

And with that, they climbed onto the little makeshift raft, pushed off into the inky black water, and vanished into the night.

Alcatraz prison was located on Alcatraz Island in the bay just off San Francisco, California.

A LIFE OF CRIME

When Frank Morris arrived at Alcatraz prison, he'd already spent most of his life in and out of trouble with the law. He was an orphan by the time he was 11 years old, convicted of his first crime at 13, and still a teenager when he was arrested for armed robbery. Morris was very smart, with an IQ higher than most people's, but he just couldn't stay out of trouble. He'd also tried to escape from other, less secure prisons many times.

John and Clarence Anglin didn't turn to bank robbery until they were in their 20s. They had tried several times to escape from the Atlanta Federal Penitentiary, which is what earned them cells in Alcatraz. Although the Anglins were born in Georgia, they'd spent time every summer in Michigan as kids, swimming in the icy waters there. It was a skill that may have helped them later.

By the time Morris and the Anglins arrived at Alcatraz, Allen West had already been in prison there for three years. After doing time at the Atlanta Federal Penitentiary, where all four men first met, West dreamed of escape. But Alcatraz was said to be 100 percent escape-proof. Thick iron bars across the front of each cell made it impossible to break out. Carefully placed guard towers more than three stories high ensured the jailers had a good view of all areas at all times.

But the main reason prisoners couldn't escape was that the cold, rough waters of the Pacific Ocean surrounded the island prison, isolating it from the rest of the world. The nearest land was more than 1.6 kilometers (1 mile) away, at Angel Island. All boats not associated with the prison had to stay at least 183 meters (600 feet) away from the island of Alcatraz. And that limit was very strictly enforced.

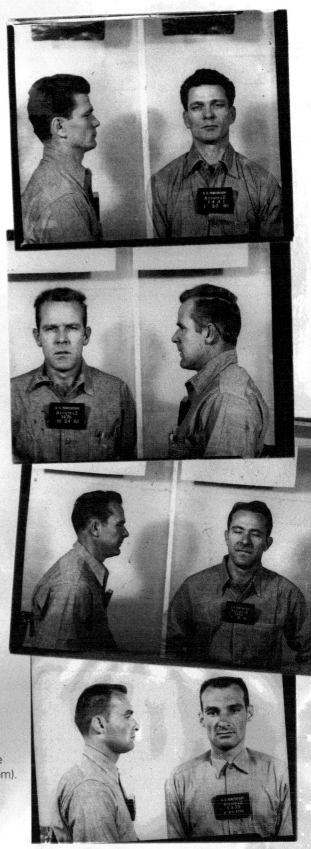

Mug shots of Alcatraz prisoners Frank Morris (top), John Anglin (second from top), his brother Clarence Anglin (second from bottom), and Allen West (bottom).

Alcatraz Prison Breakout

DREAMS OF ESCAPE

But for prisoners who had nothing but time on their hands, there was little to think about except escape. After all, they reasoned, the iron bars only blocked the front of the cell—maybe there were other exits. And the guards didn't check on the prisoners as thoroughly at night, since the criminals were securely locked in their cells.

It was probably in September 1961 that Morris, West, and the Anglins started talking about escape. Their plan began to take shape a few months later as they took advantage of

In Alcatraz prison, cells were stacked on top of each other in long rows.

situations no one could have predicted. West, who was cocky and unpopular with the guards, was often given the worst jobs around the prison. In December, he was told to clean up an area that was hardly ever used. He came across some old saw blades there and smuggled them back to his cell.

Then Morris discovered that the concrete around the air vents at the back of his cell had been softened by the damp ocean air and could be chipped away. West stole a vacuum cleaner motor while repairing a broken machine and made a drill out of it.

GOOD LUCK GETTING OUT!

Modern prisons depend on more than bars to keep prisoners from vanishing. Some inmates wear wristbands programmed with their identification and background. It's easy for guards to check these and quickly get an accurate head count. Some of these bands include radio-frequency identification-tracking technology, which allows the prison to know where a prisoner is at all times. Other prisons scan fingerprints or use biometrics (technology that analyzes such features as DNA, fingerprints, retinas, and more) to track prisoners and transfer information from one prison facility to another.

Cameras monitor prisoners and are constantly checked by guards. The cameras are often bullet proof, so they're hard to disable. Teleconferencing and videoconferencing technology have cut down the need to transfer prisoners by vehicle for court appearances, meaning they have fewer chances to make an escape from outside the actual walls of the prison.

DRILLING TO FREEDOM

The four men began using the drill to dig through the back walls of their cells. They knew that a corridor stretched behind their cells. This 0.9-meter- (3-foot-) wide passage was where the pipes and wires for water and electricity ran.

Morris and West had adjacent cells, so while Morris worked in his cell, digging at the concrete with the vacuum cleaner drill, West kept watch for the guard on patrol. Then they switched jobs. The Anglins, whose cells were also side by side, did the same. The men used periscopes made with mirrors and cardboard so they'd see the guards as soon as possible and have lots of time to cover up what they were doing.

They often worked during the music hour, when the noise of the inmates playing their instruments in their cells covered up the sounds

Here is the enlarged air vent that one of the prisoners escaped through, as well as the fake cover he constructed for it.

of digging. Morris himself even played the concertina (an accordion-like musical instrument),
but he soon found a much better use for it.

As the holes became bigger, the prisoners
made fake grilles from painted cardboard and
tobacco boxes. They put suitcases or clothes in
front of the grilles so that, at a glance, no one
could take a close look at them. By May 1962,
Morris and the Anglins had enlarged their ven-
tilation holes enough that they could squeeze
through them and leave their cells. West wasn't
far behind.

THE SECRET WORKSHOP

At night, Morris and the Anglin brothers
silently creeped along the corridor where the
pipes ran and climbed up to the top of the cell
block. They knew exactly where they were heading, thanks to West.

He had been assigned to clean and paint up
there, above a row of cells, and he made sure
he dropped as much dust as possible when he
worked. He had a plan. When the guards com-
plained about the dust, West suggested he cover
the area with blankets to prevent the dirt from
escaping. He knew that would also create a
secret workshop area where the prisoners could
work unseen and undisturbed.

This was where, in the dark of night, Morris
and the Anglins made the raft that they hoped
would transport them all to freedom. Other
prisoners supported their plan to escape by

helping them steal more than 50 waterproof raincoats. The jackets were carefully stitched, then pasted together using glue stolen from the prison's glove-making shop. The men bonded the seams together using the heat of the prison's steam pipes.

Morris and the Anglins used the raincoats to construct three pontoons (long, inflatable tubes) that would form their raft. The raft would be inflated using Morris's modified concertina. The men had no idea if the raft could support them or if it would hold together, but they were willing to take the chance. They even began work on a second raft in case they needed it.

How did the men know how to build rafts? Morris had read about it in one of the magazines he borrowed from the prison library. They made life jackets the same way. Then the trio built paddles from wood scraps that they stole and scrounged.

BREAKOUT!

The 1962 escape was the most famous attempt to break out of Alcatraz, but it wasn't the only one. In the 29 years that Alcatraz operated as a federal prison, 36 inmates made a total of 14 attempts to escape.

In December 1937, Theodore Cole and Ralph Roe filed through iron bars in the prison and escaped as the fog hid them from the guards in the watchtowers. Like Morris and the Anglins, their bodies were never found, but the severe wintry weather on the night of their escape led police to conclude they had drowned.

One of the deadliest escape attempts became known as the Battle of Alcatraz. In 1946, a group of convicts took over part of the prison before attempting to break out. Two days later, they were forced to surrender, but not before two guards and three inmates were killed.

VANISHED

Before leaving his cell, John Anglin carefully placed the papier-mâché head he'd made on the pillow on his bed. Then he slipped out the hole he'd dug just below his sink, at the far end of his cell.

UP, UP, AND AWAY

The prisoners had already made papier-mâché heads using toilet paper and paper they ripped out of magazines. The faces were carefully painted. (Some prisoners were allowed to have paints and drawing supplies in their cells.) Hair and eyebrows were added using clippings Clarence Anglin stole from the prison barbershop. The heads had already proven to be good enough to

fool the guards, who just took a brief look in each cell every night in the dim light of the night patrol.

The men had also already used the network of pipes to climb to the very top of the building and pry open the ventilator at the top of the air shaft. In case anyone examined the shaft, they'd made a fake bolt out of soap to wedge it in place. The convicts hoped it would cover their tracks and make it tough to trace their escape route. Everything was ready for the four men to escape—or so they thought.

Morris set the date and time for their escape: the night of June 11, 1962. It was a night when there'd be almost no moon and the darkness would help conceal their daring getaway. As soon as the lights were turned down in the cells, Morris and the Anglins were ready. They carefully placed the heads they had made on their pillows and pulled the sheets and blankets up around them. For the escapees to have the maximum amount of time, they had to make the fake heads look as real as possible.

Silently, each man moved the grille off the back wall of his cell and slid through the hole one last time. *But where was West?*

Prisoners on Alcatraz were constantly watched by heavily armed guards in high guard towers located throughout the island.

TOO LATE!

West was wild with frustration. He'd done all of the work on the life jackets and paddles in his cell at night, not up above in the secret workshop. He figured it would only take him a short time to enlarge the hole enough for him to slip through. But when he finally drilled out the rest of the wall—at the last minute, on the very night of the escape—he was shocked to find a metal bar blocking the hole.

While West was still trying to dig and smash his way out of the back of his cell, the other three made the tough decision to leave him behind. West finally got out and made his way to the roof. But in the darkness, he didn't see the mostly completed life raft, paddle, and life jacket that had been left for him.

Meanwhile, Morris and the Anglins were making their way across the roof with a raft, paddles, and life jackets tucked under their arms. The bright light from the prison guard tower pierced the night as it swept over the island. The escapees dodged and ducked, trying to avoid it.

Soon they were at the edge of the roof. From there, they shimmied down the four-story-high bakery smokestack, carefully climbed over the prison's barbed-wire fence, and crept to the northeast edge of the island. There the men worked desperately to inflate their raft and life jackets. Then they slipped into the water—and into one of the biggest mysteries ever.

DISAPPEARED DESPERADOS

No one knows for certain what happened to famous criminals Robert Leroy Parker and Harry Alonzo Longabaugh, better known as Butch Cassidy and the Sundance Kid. The duo robbed banks and trains across the United States in the late 1800s, but when detectives were closing in, they escaped to Bolivia, South America.

But Butch and Sundance just couldn't give up their thieving ways. In November 1908, they robbed a bank in southern Bolivia and were killed in a gunfight—apparently. Their bodies were never definitely identified, and none of the bodies in the cemetery where they were supposedly buried have DNA matching their relatives' DNA.

A number of people, including a doctor and a rancher friend, claimed Cassidy visited them after he was supposedly shot. His sister says he died in 1937—but she won't say where he's buried because people might then disturb his final resting place.

Robbers Robert Leroy Parker (left) and Harry Alonzo Longabaugh (right) were better known as Butch Cassidy and the Sundance Kid.

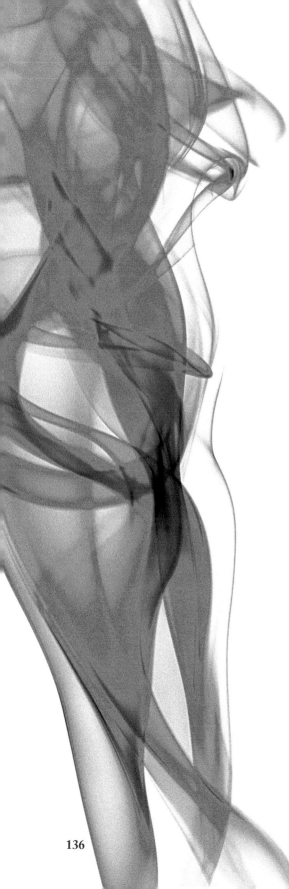

JAILBREAK!

"Morris! Morris! Get up," yelled the guard into Frank Morris's cell the next morning.

When Morris didn't even move, the guard reached into the cell and slapped the side of his head. Morris's head rolled off the side of the bed!

The guard yelled again—in sheer fright—and then realized the head on the floor was fake. That's when he got really scared: Where was Morris? The guard shouted for help and raced to the nearest phone to sound the alarm.

A fast cell check quickly told the guards that Morris wasn't the only convict missing—the Anglin brothers were gone too! Sirens wailed as guards scoured the island looking for the three escaped men.

West had spent the night on the prison roof trying to decide what to do. By the time the breakout was discovered, West was back in his cell, probably trying to keep a low profile. But when a papier-mâché head and other incriminating evidence was found in his cell, he was forced to give the Federal Bureau of Investigation (FBI) agents and prison officials details about the escape plan. Perhaps he hoped it would reduce the length of his time in Alcatraz, or maybe he wanted to make it sound as if he was the mastermind of the escape. But in fact, he may have deliberately given the authorities incorrect information, to help his buddies get away.

Alcatraz Island is just 2.4 kilometers (1.5 miles) offshore from the city of San Francisco.

FOLLOW THE FOOTPRINTS

Prison officers and the FBI immediately began searching for Morris and the Anglins. They knew it was possible that the convicts had paddled the more than 1.6 kilometers (1 mile) from Alcatraz to Angel Island, a much larger island but with a sparse population. However, the police thought that the cold water, which would have been only about 10°C (50°F), and ocean tides made this unlikely. As well, the escapees would have to either steal a boat or use their raft again to get off Angel Island.

At first, the FBI reported there was no trace of the men after they left Alcatraz. But evidence was later revealed that showed footprints leading away from the raft had been found on Angel Island. As well, a blue Chevrolet was stolen in nearby Marin County the day after the escape. Could this be the getaway car? On June 13, a man called the police complaining about a similar car that had forced him off the road in the area. Inside, he said, had been three men, although he wasn't able to see them clearly enough to give a description of them.

Boat operators in the bay were told to be on the lookout for the men or any strange items found floating in the water. Two days after the escape, a packet of letters and photos turned up that belonged to the Anglins. A raft, homemade paddle, and life jacket were discovered on a beach on Angel Island. But there was no sign of Morris or the Anglin brothers, no matter how hard the crews searched.

REENACTING THE DARING ESCAPE

In 2003, the television show *MythBusters* examined the story of the escape from Alcatraz. Based on information from police reports, the hosts built a raft similar to the one made by the escapees. Then they paddled off into the chilly night.

The MythBusters hosts didn't make it to Angel Island, but they did safely reach the Marin Headlands, on the other side of the Golden Gate Bridge, north of San Francisco. Although the original raft, lifejacket, and paddle had been found on Angel Island the day after the escape, the television show speculated they might have been carried there by the current.

MythBusters also investigated the packet of photos that was dropped by the escaping convicts, as if by accident. It might actually have been a deliberate move by the prisoners to put authorities off their trail—Morris was very smart. If the prisoners knew the timing of the tides, they could have released the package at just the right moment so the water would carry it where they wanted the officers to think they were going—but Morris and the Anglins may have been headed in a totally different direction.

TECHNOLOGY: FRIEND OR FOE?

Today, a prisoner can use a cell phone that's been smuggled into prison to plan his escape with accomplices who are on the outside. Once out, a computer can help him plan his next move. But all of that technology leaves traces that police can follow to track down the escaped prisoner. Officials can locate cell phones or use eye or voice recognition software to positively identify a convict. They may also use infrared cameras mounted on helicopters to find an escaped prisoner in a forest or heavy bush. And sometimes low-tech works just as well—police still use sniffer dogs to track down escapees.

MYSTERIOUS MOURNERS

A cousin of Morris and his daughter both claim to have met up with him after his escape. Their stories couldn't be confirmed, but they helped keep alive the legend of the daring breakout. Other family members claimed to have received postcards from the men.

Relatives of the Anglins said the brothers' mother often received flowers delivered with no card saying who had sent them. Could it be her sons? The family also told a story of two very tall women wearing heavy makeup who attended the funeral of the brothers' mother, Rachel, in 1973. The pair spoke to no one—were they afraid their low voices would give away their true identities?—and disappeared as soon as the service was over.

The Anglin family believes the brothers made it to Brazil. They supposedly sent a secret message to their older brother, a prisoner in an Alabama jail, to join them, but he was electrocuted on the jail's fence when he tried to escape in 1964.

WHO WAS THE MASTERMIND?

West later took much of the credit for master-minding the escape, but he may have been just bragging—he was known for his arrogance. If he was angry at his friends for leaving him behind, he may have told the authorities everything he knew in hopes that the escapees would soon be behind bars again just like him.

On the other hand, as mentioned earlier, West may have passed on false information to help his friends. West reported that the escapees had no plans beyond getting as far away from San Francisco as possible, but who knows whether he would have given away their real schemes even if he did know what they were.

Since the men's bodies were never found, they may have safely escaped, although it is common for people who die in San Francisco Bay's icy waters never to be found. The tides carry bodies out to the vast Pacific Ocean. The FBI also said that the cold water would have greatly hindered the men's ability to paddle, swim, or even think straight after just 20 minutes of exposure.

The FBI distributed wanted posters for each of the Anglin brothers and for Frank Morris.

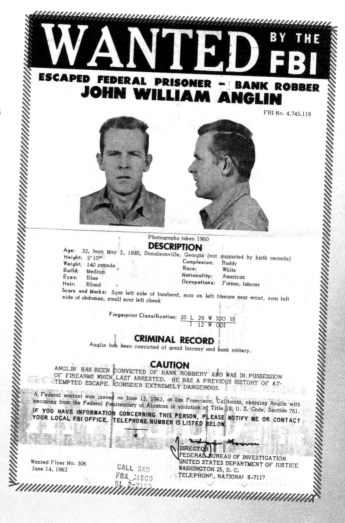

WANTED BY THE FBI

ESCAPED FEDERAL PRISONER – BANK ROBBER
JOHN WILLIAM ANGLIN

FBI No. 4,745,119

Photographs taken 1960

DESCRIPTION

Age: 32, born May 2, 1930, Donalsonville, Georgia (not supported by birth records)
Height: 5'10"
Weight: 140 pounds
Build: Medium
Eyes: Blue
Hair: Blond
Complexion: Ruddy
Race: White
Nationality: American
Occupations: Farmer, laborer
Scars and Marks: Scar left side of forehead, scar on left forearm near wrist, scar left side of abdomen, small scar left cheek

Fingerprint Classification: 20 L 29 W 100 18
I 12 W OOI

CRIMINAL RECORD

Anglin has been convicted of grand larceny and bank robbery.

CAUTION

ANGLIN HAS BEEN CONVICTED OF BANK ROBBERY AND WAS IN POSSESSION OF FIREARMS WHEN LAST ARRESTED. HE HAS A PREVIOUS HISTORY OF ATTEMPTED ESCAPE. CONSIDER EXTREMELY DANGEROUS.

A Federal warrant was issued on June 13, 1962, at San Francisco, California, charging Anglin with escaping from the Federal Penitentiary at Alcatraz in violation of Title 18, U. S. Code, Section 751.

IF YOU HAVE INFORMATION CONCERNING THIS PERSON, PLEASE NOTIFY ME OR CONTACT YOUR LOCAL FBI OFFICE. TELEPHONE NUMBER IS LISTED BELOW.

DIRECTOR
FEDERAL BUREAU OF INVESTIGATION
UNITED STATES DEPARTMENT OF JUSTICE
WASHINGTON 25, D. C.
TELEPHONE, NATIONAL 8-7117

Wanted Flyer No. 306
June 14, 1962

CALL SAN FRANCISCO
KL 2-7900

ONE BODY, UNIDENTIFIED

Another theory concerns a body that was found in the San Francisco Bay a little more than a month after the prison break. The body had deteriorated too much to be identified. The clothing was bleached by the water and the sun, but it seemed to be similar in colors and design to the Alcatraz prisoner uniforms.

The FBI checked its records and found that no one had been reported missing who had been wearing clothes like that. So who was it? Did the Anglin brothers decide they'd be better off on their own, murder Morris, and push him off the raft? Did one of the men fall off the raft and get swept away? But the body could never be definitely identified using the scientific methods of the time.

JOHN "BONES" DOE

About eight months after the escape, human bones were found off Point Reyes, about 50 kilometers (31 miles) west-northwest of San Francisco. Could the currents have swept the body of one of the convicts here? The body was buried in a local cemetery under the name John "Bones" Doe, but first it was thoroughly examined and notes were carefully recorded.

Scientists reviewed those notes decades later and found that the examiner had estimated the dead man was 171 centimeters (67.5 inches) tall. That was exactly Frank Morris's height! So the body was dug up and genetic material from it was compared to that of a relative from Morris's father's family.

However, the DNA samples didn't match and the scientists had to conclude the body wasn't Morris's.

Based on the height estimate, the bones are unlikely to belong to either John or Clarence Anglin, so the question of the whereabouts of the trio of men remains unanswered.

WHERE ARE THEY NOW?

The FBI officially closed its case on the Alcatraz escapees on December 31, 1979, stating that the prisoners had drowned. One reason people think the three must have died is because the only way the trio had known to make money before their time in Alcatraz was to rob or steal. Yet they were never caught after their escape. Could they have resisted the temptation to turn to crime again?

However, Morris and the Anglins are still on the U.S. Marshals Service list of wanted criminals, and the officers continue to encourage people to call in with any tips they might have to help them solve the case. As Deputy U.S. Marshal Michael Dyke said in 2009, "There's no proof they're dead, so we're not going to quit looking."

There were members of Morris's and the Anglins' families who hoped the men would return to Alcatraz on the fiftieth anniversary of

U.S. Marshals created this wanted poster for Frank Morris. The top photo shows how he looked in 1962 when he escaped Alcatraz. The lower image illustrates how he might have looked in 2014 when, if he was still alive, he would have been 88 years old.

WANTED By U.S. MARSHALS

U.S. Department of Justice
United States Marshals Service

Name: MORRIS,FRANK LEE
Alias: CLARK,CARL CECIL; LAINE,FRANK; LANE,FRANK

Sex .... MALE
Race .... WHITE OR WHITE HISPANIC
Date of Birth 09/01/1926
Place of Birth .... District of Columbia
Height .... 5'08"
Weight .... 135 pounds
Eyes .... Hazel
Hair .... Gray/Partially Gray
Skintone .... Ruddy
Scars/Tattoos .... Removed Tattoo on Forehead; Scar Arm, Left Upper; Scar Arm, Left, Nonspecific; Scar Elbow, Left

AGE: 88 YEARS OLD AS OF 2014
FRANK MORRIS IS WANTED FOR THE JUNE 11, 1962 ESCAPE FROM THE FEDERAL PENITENTIARY AT ALCATRAZ IN SAN FRANCISCO CALIFORNIA. MORRIS WAS SENTENCED ON SEPTEMBER 19, 1956 TO 14 YEARS CUSTODY FOR A BANK BURGLARY IN SLIDELL LOUISIANA.
SECOND PHOTO AGE PROGRESSED TO AGE 88.
AGE PROGRESSION RENDERING COURTESY FEDERAL BUREAU OF INVESTIGATION

AUTHORITY: DONALD M O'KEEFE
UNITED STATES MARSHAL
NORTHERN DISTRICT OF CALIFORNIA

http://www.usdoj.gov/marshals

NOTICE TO ARRESTING AGENCY: Before arrest, validate warrant through National Crime Information Center (NCIC). If arrested or whereabouts known, contact the nearest United States Marshals Office or call the United States Marshals Service Headquarters at 1-877-926-8332.

These photos show Clarence Anglin (top) in 1962 and how he might have looked in 2014. His brother John is shown in the lower two pictures.

their escape. On June 11, 2012, people gathered on the site of the old prison, hoping for a glimpse of the men. But if they were there, they didn't make themselves known to anyone.

In 2014, researchers' high-tech computer models used hydraulics (the science of moving water) and virtual vessels to show that the winds and tides in San Francisco Bay on the night Morris and the Anglins escaped meant it was unlikely they made it to land. But they also showed that if the trio left Alcatraz very close to midnight, the tides would have flowed in exactly the right direction for them. The model predicted that the abandoned raft, paddles, and life jackets would have floated back into the bay, toward Angel Island, which is exactly where the FBI found them.

The U.S. Marshals Service won't officially end its search for the escapees until one hundred years after their births, which will happen in 2031. The Anglins' family thinks the brothers escaped to Brazil and believes there is a photo that proves it. Until definite evidence is discovered to prove Frank Morris and the Anglins died in the icy waters around Alcatraz, many people will continue to believe that they escaped—and vanished.

"THE ROCK"

Because the island was rocky, with almost no plant or animal life, and it was a bleak and rough place to stay, prisoners called Alcatraz "The Rock." Alcatraz prison closed in 1963 and today is one of San Francisco's most popular tourist destinations.

Alcatraz has also captured the popular imagination as one of the most haunted places in the United States. Mysterious screams, strange crashing noises, and echoing footsteps have all been described as coming from the empty cells.

The Escape from Alcatraz Triathlon held in San Francisco each year in June—the month Morris and the Anglins escaped—begins with a grueling swim from Alcatraz Island. People have talked about turning the island into a park or shopping center—or even a hotel, college, or the site of a monument to match the Statue of Liberty on America's east coast!

Today, crowds of tourists take a ferry from San Francisco to Alcatraz Island to tour the former prison.

HOT ON THE TRAIL

Every year, thousands of adults go missing. Police officials don't have an exact number because many are never reported. You might think most of those who disappear are criminals, but actually, many people abandon their lives because of family pressures, financial problems, or just a desire to reinvent themselves.

Disappearing isn't easy, but staying hidden is even tougher. For instance, you need more than one piece of identification to apply for a job or open a bank account, and it's illegal to use or possess any false identity document.

To make sure they're not found, people who want to vanish have to stay away from friends and family. Detectives know that most people in hiding eventually crave contact with someone they knew for a long time, so investigators keep likely targets under surveillance. Police also keep an eye on places where the vanished person liked to hang out, because they know many people can't shake old habits.

There are many closed-circuit television (CCTV) cameras located throughout cities that can provide evidence about a missing person.

To stay hidden, a missing person has to be careful not to earn any speeding or parking tickets. If they do, their identification information is entered into the legal system and is easily tracked. Medical, dental, and school records are another tool private investigators use to find missing people.

Detectives try to think like the escaped criminal or missing person to figure out where the person is and where she'll go next. GPS-enabled cell phones, cell phone triangulation (tracking radio signals between several network radio towers and the phone), and phone logs (lists of calls made or received) can all provide clues. Electronic bank transactions and clues on social networking sites often yield key information to investigators.

Closed-circuit television (CCTV) cameras in public places record photographic evidence of a person's location, as well as the date and time she was there. An unmanned aerial vehicle (UAV), or drone, can fly over wilderness areas that are difficult to access otherwise. Not only can these flying machines find people who are trying to hide, but they can also locate those stranded by avalanches or plane crashes.

This eagle is fitted with a Global Positioning System (GPS) transmitter. It collects data, then sends it to a computer server via mobile phone networks.

Researchers can monitor the footage from hundreds of CCTV cameras in hopes of discovering a clue about a missing person.

THEFT AT THE GARDNER MUSEUM

FAMOUS ART GONE FOREVER?

"Give up on the stupid flag," hissed one of the thieves to the other. "We gotta get outta here. You're never gonna get that thing out of the frame."

"All right, all right," said the second thief, "but I wanna take something. I'm gonna grab this eagle off the top."

"Hey, look, it's a picture of the old dame who made this party possible. Think we should lift it too?"

"Forget it, it's too big. Look, let's just take these drawings and get outta here."

"Watch it! You just broke that! C'mon, let's go."

Grunting and gasping, the thieves carried armfuls of paintings and other items down to the side entrance where they'd come in.

"Before we go," said the first thief with a sneer, "I've got a little computer work to do." He strode over to the security room, kicked in the door, and grabbed the videotape from the recorder. The other thief ripped

the computer printout from the motion detector machine and crumpled it into the front of his jacket.

Light rain was falling on the sidewalk outside. The thieves dashed back and forth from the door of the museum to their rusty hatchback, loading in all 13 pieces of valuable art. Then they climbed in. The car's engine roared to life, and they vanished into the wet, dark night.

This gilded bronze eagle that the thieves stole is about 25 centimeters (10 inches) tall.

The Isabella Stewart Gardner Museum

WILD NIGHT IN THE CITY

St. Patrick's Day in 1990 was a typical wild event in Boston, Massachusetts. Boston has a lot of people with Irish heritage, so March 17 is a big day to celebrate and have a good time. Despite the light rain, people had stayed out late that Saturday night.

In contrast, it seemed like a regular quiet night at the Isabella Stewart Gardner Museum. The art gallery, near downtown Boston, was closed for the day, and guard Rick Abath was at the main security desk. One of the regular night guards had called in sick, so Abath's partner that evening was on night duty for the first time. The two took turns walking the floors of the four-story building.

In addition to the guards, there was also a surveillance system with four video monitors showing various rooms of the museum. The galleries and corridors in the museum were wired with motion detectors. If anything disturbed them, they sent a silent alarm to a computer system behind the main security desk.

Around 1:00 a.m., the fire alarm sounded! The guards raced up the stairs but eventually decided it had been a false alarm, as their investigation found no sign of fire or any other trouble. But then, a short time later, at 1:24 a.m. on March 18, true chaos broke out.

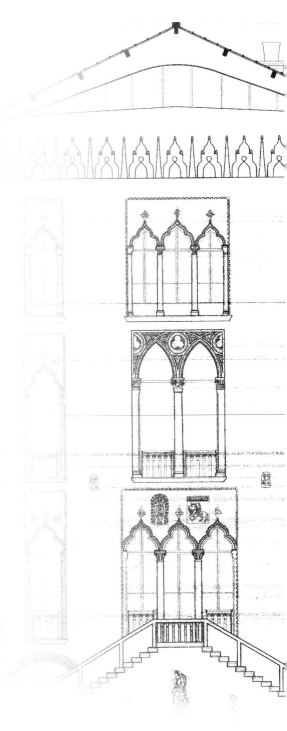

Cross-section plan of the four stories of the Isabella Stewart Gardner Museum.

CALL THE POLICE!

"It's the police! Let us in," ordered a uniformed man pressing the buzzer at the side entrance. "We're here about a disturbance on the museum's grounds." Abath quickly buzzed him in, as well as the officer with him.

Abath had been told never to let in anyone unknown when the museum was closed, but since it was the police demanding entrance, he figured he'd better do as they requested. He knew there had been some violent crimes in the area, so he was glad to have the police there to make sure everything was secure. That was his first mistake.

"Any other guards on duty?" asked the first officer.

"Yes, sir, one," replied Abath. "He's upstairs doing his rounds."

"Well, you'd better call him down too."

Abath called down the other guard. As Abath and the officers stood waiting for the second guard, they chatted casually across the desk. Then the first officer looked at Abath sternly.

"You look familiar," he said. "I think we've got a warrant out for you. Come here and show me some identification." That's when the guard made his second mistake.

The Isabella Stewart Gardner Museum is a world-class art gallery. It includes important European, Asian, and American works of art.

HANDCUFFED AND GAGGED

Abath knew there were no warrants out for his arrest, but he thought he had to obey the officer. When he walked toward the men, he moved out from behind his desk and away from the museum's only alarm button, which could send a direct alert to a Boston police station.

As soon as Abath was away from the alarm, the police officers handcuffed him. The second guard arrived then and was also quickly handcuffed. That's when Abath noticed the policemen's uniforms didn't look quite right. A closer look told him their mustaches seemed fake too.

"Wait, why are you arresting me?" asked the second guard.

"This is no arrest," said the burglar, grinning. "It's a robbery. Don't give us any trouble and you won't get hurt."

The thieves wrapped the guards' hands, feet, and mouths with duct tape, led them down to the basement, and handcuffed them to pipes far away from each other. Then they headed upstairs to begin looting the museum, confident there'd be no guards or police to stop them.

The thieves took just 81 minutes to comb through the galleries. After a quick stop at the museum's security room to remove all traces of their visit (or so they thought), they were back out the door. The museum is close to a highway, so perhaps, after a quick stop to change cars in case anyone saw them leave the gallery, it wasn't long before the thieves were far away, taking the paintings and other items with them.

A few days after the theft, a security guard protects the Dutch Room (shown here behind police tape). From this gallery alone, the thieves stole four paintings, an etching, and an ancient bronze vase.

A GREAT ART COLLECTOR

Isabella Stewart Gardner was an American art collector and one of the most important female patrons of the arts in the United States. When her art collection grew too big for her home, she decided to create a museum to share her treasures with everyone. The museum opened in 1903 with a reception that included champagne—and donuts.

The Concert by Johannes Vermeer, one of the stolen paintings, was Gardner's first major purchase. She was also the first American to own paintings by art superstars Sandro Botticelli (1445–1510) and Henri Matisse (1869–1954).

Want to visit the museum for free? Not a problem if your name is Isabella or it's your birthday. As well, Gardner was a big fan of the Boston Red Sox baseball team, so even today, visitors with Red Sox souvenirs enter the gallery at a discount.

Isabella Stewart Gardner was 48 when this portrait was painted.

ALARM AROUND THE WORLD

No one knew anything about the robbery until much later that morning when a maintenance worker rang the museum's doorbell and no security guard came to let him in. A few minutes later, one of the guards for the next shift arrived. The worker and the guard rang the bell again and again and knocked loudly on the windows.

When they still got no answer, the pair called a supervisor, who quickly arrived. He used his key to open up. As soon as he saw a broken picture frame on the floor and the smashed door of the security room, he called police.

With guns drawn, the officers—authentic ones this time—crept carefully down the halls. They had

A hallway on the first floor of the Isabella Stewart Gardner Museum.

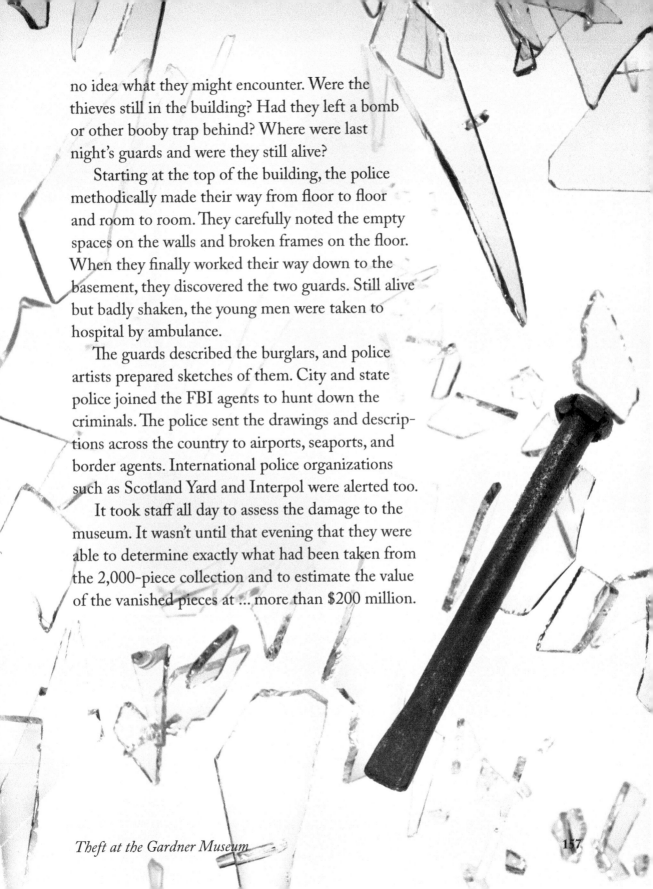

no idea what they might encounter. Were the thieves still in the building? Had they left a bomb or other booby trap behind? Where were last night's guards and were they still alive?

Starting at the top of the building, the police methodically made their way from floor to floor and room to room. They carefully noted the empty spaces on the walls and broken frames on the floor. When they finally worked their way down to the basement, they discovered the two guards. Still alive but badly shaken, the young men were taken to hospital by ambulance.

The guards described the burglars, and police artists prepared sketches of them. City and state police joined the FBI agents to hunt down the criminals. The police sent the drawings and descriptions across the country to airports, seaports, and border agents. International police organizations such as Scotland Yard and Interpol were alerted too.

It took staff all day to assess the damage to the museum. It wasn't until that evening that they were able to determine exactly what had been taken from the 2,000-piece collection and to estimate the value of the vanished pieces at ... more than $200 million.

SEEKING INFORMATION
BY THE FBI

The FBI is seeking information in the theft of thirteen works of art from the Isabella Stewart Gardner Museum in 1990.

The Concert
VERMEER, 1658 - 1660
Oil on canvas, 72.5 x 64.7 cm

$5 Million Reward

The FBI encourages anyone who may have information on the whereabouts of the artwork to contact the FBI at 1-800-CALL-FBI or submit online at Tips.FBI.Gov.

WORLD-FAMOUS ARTWORKS

The Gardner Museum staff determined that 13 pieces were missing:

◊ *The Concert*, a painting by Johannes Vermeer
◊ *A Lady and Gentleman in Black*, a painting by Rembrandt van Rijn (known as Rembrandt)
◊ *The Storm on the Sea of Galilee*, another painting by Rembrandt
◊ A self-portrait (etching) by Rembrandt
◊ *Chez Tortoni*, a painting by Édouard Manet
◊ *Landscape with an Obelisk*, a painting by Govaert Flinck
◊ Five sketches by Edgar Dégas
◊ A Chinese bronze vase, or beaker, called a Ku, that was more than 3,000 years old
◊ A finial (small, ornamental cap) shaped like an eagle from a flag associated with the great French leader Napoleon Bonaparte

A number of the paintings were especially valuable and unusual. *The Concert,* painted between 1658 and 1660, shows a man playing a lute (a stringed instrument), a woman playing a harpsichord (a type of early keyboard), and a woman singing. It is one of only 34 known works by Vermeer, a Dutch painter famous for the way he portrayed light.

He was one of the greatest painters of the 1600s, known as the Golden Age in the Netherlands. *The Concert* alone is today worth about $200 million, which makes it the most valuable unrecovered stolen painting ever. Rembrandt's *The Storm on the Sea of Galilee* was painted in 1633. Rembrandt is considered one of the greatest European painters and the most important Dutch artist ever. His works are all extremely valuable.

The other stolen pieces were important too. For instance, Manet was famous as one of the first artists of the 1800s to paint scenes from modern daily life. And while Dégas was

DON'T DROP THAT!

Works of art can be badly damaged when they are stolen. Art lovers were horrified to hear that when the thieves stole Rembrandt's *The Storm on the Sea of Galilee*, they hacked it out of the frame. After another theft, a masterpiece was damaged beyond repair when the thief rolled it up and sat on it: the canvas cracked and the paint flaked off.

Many pieces of art are kept in rooms that are carefully monitored for the correct temperature and humidity to ensure the works won't deteriorate. But when paintings are stolen, they may be hidden in hot, dry attics or cold, wet basements. Some museums exhibit their masterpieces in rooms with low lighting to protect them from fading. When art is stolen, it may be exposed to very bright light, which can cause irreparable damage.

The Storm on the Sea of Galilee was one of the three works of art by Rembrandt that the thieves stole.

well known as a founder of the now-popular school of art known as Impressionism, the sketches that the thieves took were not nearly as valuable as many other works in the gallery. Police were stumped—had the thieves snatched them in a fit of anger when they weren't able to take the nearby Napoleonic flag?

CLUES ON THE HARD DRIVE?

The police were able to retrace the thieves' movements for the entire time they were in the museum. For instance, they knew the thieves had gone down to the basement twice to make sure the guards were still securely held by the duct tape.

How did the police have so much information about the robbers? Although the young guard Rick Abath had made mistakes, the thieves made one too. When they removed the records from the security room, they didn't realize their movements had already been captured directly onto the security computer's hard drive.

The motion detectors, which sent signals to the hard drive, had been installed to keep people from getting too close to fragile paintings or touching them. The thieves were likely even startled by one when they removed the first painting from the wall. The monitoring device was found thrown to the floor, a pile of smashed parts.

The hard drive provided police with a lot of information about the thieves' movements. Officers knew the burglars had spent a lot of time in the room that held the Napoleonic flag. When they examined the banner, they could see that the eagle that had adorned the top of the flagpole was missing, and that the glass and wood of the frame was damaged where the thieves had tried to remove it.

SUSPECT #1 (MUSTACHE)

SUSPECT #2 (MUSTACHE)

SUSPECT #1 (NO MUSTACHE)

SUSPECT #2 (NO MUSTACHE)

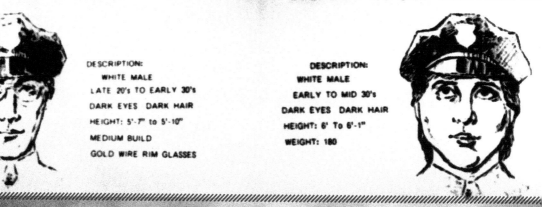

DESCRIPTION:
WHITE MALE
LATE 20's TO EARLY 30's
DARK EYES DARK HAIR
HEIGHT: 5'-7" to 5'-10"
MEDIUM BUILD
GOLD WIRE RIM GLASSES

DESCRIPTION:
WHITE MALE
EARLY TO MID 30's
DARK EYES DARK HAIR
HEIGHT: 6' To 6'-1"
WEIGHT: 180

Three days after the theft, the FBI released these sketches of the robbery suspects. Since guard Rick Abath thought their mustaches looked fake, the suspects are shown with and without them.

HUNTING FOR CLUES

For three days, police and FBI specialists searched the museum for scraps of clothing and hair, combed the floors for footprints, and dusted for fingerprints to try to find any evidence that would help them identify the thieves. Shards of glass showed where the thieves had smashed paintings out of their frames. Another Rembrandt self-portrait lay abandoned on the floor. It looked as if the thieves had tried to remove the wooden panel from its heavy frame. In another room lay the broken frames from two of the Dégas sketches they stole.

Police found flecks of oil paint and pieces of canvas from where the thieves had ripped with knives, hammers, and chisels to slash some of the world's most famous paintings out of their gilt frames. But they had no clues about where the paintings and thieves were now. It was as if they had all vanished.

ALARMING INFORMATION

Detectives figure the thieves used women to case the gallery. Why women? They blend in better in art galleries, where there are usually many more female visitors than males. They would have located the paintings that were to be stolen and probably made notes about their placement and how they were secured.

Investigators also know that criminals carefully study, or "case," buildings they intend to rob. In the case of the Gardner Museum, they likely spent time assessing the museum's security. Information such as how many guards patrolled at night and what the shifts were would have helped them decide when to enter the gallery.

Perhaps one of the thieves or his henchmen struck up a casual conversation with a guard who was standing in the gallery. Likely, the thieves somehow learned that the only alarm to sound outside the gallery was located behind the guard's desk. The guards who may have shared this information with what seemed like curious gallery visitors would certainly have had no idea that the people planned to return for an illegal after-hours visit.

Today if you visit the Isabella Stewart Gardner Museum, you'll see empty frames where the stolen art hung. The one on the left surrounded *A Lady and Gentleman in Black*, while the one the right was around *The Storm on the Sea of Galilee* (shown on page 160).

There was no reason to think that any of the Gardner museum staff were involved in the robbery, which can sometimes happen. Still, was it just a coincidence that one of the regular guards had called in sick that night so that one of the only two guards on duty was a rookie?

Police have offered a reward of up to $5 million to anyone who could offer them information that would lead to the arrest of the thieves or the recovery of the artwork. Officers received hundreds of tips from people ranging from art dealers to prison inmates, who were perhaps hoping to trade information for reduced sentences. But the artwork seemed to have disappeared completely.

WHO WERE THE THIEVES?

Were there more than two thieves involved in the robbery? The guards reported seeing only the pair of fake policemen, but there could have been other robbers. It would have made sense to have an accomplice watching the museum entrance while the thieves were in the gallery snatching art, and maybe having another ready to drive the getaway car. The robbery took place in a time before cell phones were widely used, but a group of thieves could have depended on radios to keep in touch.

One American expert in stolen art suggested that the way the thieves operated marks them as Europeans, not Americans. American-style robberies tend to be more violent and involve guns. Tricking a guard with disguises and careful planning are characteristics of robberies in Europe. If this is true, the robbers may have driven immediately to an airport and quickly dispatched the paintings to Europe. The police have pursued leads as far away as Japan and Italy.

But the way the thieves hacked the art out of the frames and tossed other pieces on the floor marks them as inexperienced, according to one crime expert. That could mean the burglars hadn't arranged a buyer ahead of time. Perhaps the thieves hid or buried the art and are waiting for interest in the case to die down. That could take a very long time.

Another theory is that the thieves were simply thugs for hire. They were handed a floor plan and a list of what to steal, and they didn't know anything else about what was in the gallery. Once the robbers got in the gallery, they may have decided to help themselves to a few more pieces. Since the Rembrandt self-portrait was barely larger than a postage stamp, and the eagle and vase were also small, the robbers may have grabbed these, thinking they could easily sell or trade them.

Police have likely even examined the duct tape used to tie up the security guards in case there was any of the thieves' sweat on it. Any fluid could be sampled for DNA and the genetic material analyzed and matched for identification. The United States maintains a database of 7 million DNA samples from convicted criminals, so it's easy to compare DNA from crime scenes when trying to identify a criminal. As technology changes and advances, police continue to reexamine any evidence from the Gardner theft in hopes it will yield useful clues.

THE *MONA LISA*

Perhaps the most famous case of art theft involves one of the world's best-known paintings, the *Mona Lisa* by Leonardo da Vinci. On August 21, 1911, Vincenzo Peruggia, who was an employee of the Louvre museum in Paris where the painting was exhibited, hid in a broom closet. He waited until the gallery closed, then he took the painting off the wall. Peruggia hid it under his coat—it's only 77 centimeters x 53 centimeters (30 inches x 21 inches)—and walked out of the museum.

Peruggia was Italian and felt the painting should be displayed in a museum in Italy, since that was its painter's home country. The thief hid the painting for two years, but then he tried to sell it to an Italian gallery and was caught. The *Mona Lisa* was returned to the Louvre, where you can see it today.

In this depiction of the crime, an artist drew the *Mona Lisa* much larger than it actually is and showed two thieves to make the theft more dramatic.

WHO STOLE THE ART?

On March 18, 2013, the twenty-third anniversary of the robbery at the Gardner Museum, the FBI announced that it knew who had stolen the gallery's masterpieces. However, it would not give any names and said it had not been able to capture the burglars. Journalists have guessed the identity of the thieves based on their resemblances to the sketches police artists produced according to the guards' descriptions. But the FBI won't release any information until it has the criminals in custody.

The stolen art still hasn't been recovered, either, the police admit. Pursuing rumors and hints, they were able to follow the paintings until about the year 2000, when they reached Philadelphia and then vanished. Detectives are certain the theft was carried out by a crime group based in New England.

At today's values, the missing artwork is thought to be worth about $500 million. Experts still wonder why the Gardner thieves passed up so many even more valuable paintings or small, easy-to-carry art objects. Some of the paintings that were stolen are so famous and recognizable that no one could ever safely display, sell, or trade them. One expert said the paintings had no value to the thieves because they were so well known, and he predicted they would soon be found abandoned. Sadly, he was wrong. The FBI says only 5 percent of stolen art is ever returned. But since there are so few buyers for such recognizable pieces, the chances of getting back the Gardner works might be as high as 20 percent.

Visitors to the gallery see empty frames in the places where the paintings once hung. This reminds people that the collection is still incomplete and show where the works will appear when they are returned. The empty frames indicate the museum's hope that the paintings *will* come back.

Staff are not allowed to replace the missing paintings with other art. According to Isabella Stewart Gardner's will, changes, such as replacing stolen art, cannot be made to the gallery.

MANY MISSING MASTERPIECES

Just as thieves took advantage of the St. Patrick's Day festivities to rob the Gardner Museum, other robbers stole a masterpiece from the Ashmolean Museum in Oxford, England, on New Year's Eve 1999. As fireworks welcomed the new millennium, burglars stole a painting by Paul Cézanne worth about $5 million.

In some cases of art theft, the thieves have been arrested but the paintings have never been recovered. Some robbers claim to have burned the paintings they stole to destroy evidence. One said he panicked and tossed the painting he pilfered into the garbage.

There's still hope that the works stolen from the Isabella Stewart Gardner Museum will one day be returned. In 2014, a famous missing painting by Pierre-Auguste Renoir was returned to the Baltimore Museum of Art—it had gone missing 63 years earlier!

THE SEARCH GOES ON

The FBI announced in March 2013 that it thought it knew who the two thieves were who stole the artwork from the Gardner Museum, but didn't state their names. It's believed the thieves died many years ago. The agency also disclosed that the stolen works of art had been transported using underground crime channels from Boston through Connecticut to Philadelphia. According to the FBI, some of the art may have been sold there in the early 2000s.

Then in August 2015, the FBI released a never-before-seen video recorded the night before the Gardner robbery. The tape seems to show Richard Abath, the security guard on duty the night of the theft, buzzing a man into the museum. Now police wonder if this was a rehearsal for the robbery. It appears Abath was involved, but immediately after the crime he passed two lie-detector tests about his part in the theft.

Unfortunately, the visitor isn't easy to identify from the video. Police say someone has come forward saying he knows who the man is, but there are still many questions about the video. It's now available online for anyone to see.

The Gardner Museum heist is the largest in American history. So many years have passed since the heist that anyone involved could no longer be charged with the robbery. As Anthony Amore, the museum's director of security, said in 2013: "Twenty-three years since the robbery, that's far too long. It's time for these paintings to come home."

ARTNAPPING

Art is usually stolen for resale or for ransom (sometimes called artnapping). When art is sold on the black market, its value is only about 3 to 10 percent of its actual value. So the Vermeer stolen from the Gardner Museum and worth $200 million would earn a thief only about $20 million. The international market for stolen art and ancient pieces is worth about $5 billion each year.

On average, it takes five to seven years to recover stolen art. The more famous the painting, the more likely it will be returned, since it would be very hard to sell. Groups like the Art Loss Register (ALR) and the International Foundation for Art Research (IFAR) are improving the odds of recovering stolen art. These organizations maintain databases to provide information on missing masterpieces to police forces, art collectors, dealers, museums, and insurers around the world.

DETECTING FORGERIES

If the paintings stolen from the Gardner Museum are ever returned, they'll be examined carefully to make sure they actually are the stolen paintings and not forgeries. Carbon dating can be used to estimate the age of most paintings and other objects and determine whether they are old masterpieces or modern copies. This process involves measuring the amount of radiocarbon, a radioactive variety of the element carbon, in an object to calculate its age.

One way a forger may try to get around this is to obtain a canvas and frame from an unimportant painting dating from the right time period and paint over it. However, X-rays can reveal the underpainting, and so can processes known as ultraviolet fluorescence (exposing the art to ultraviolet light) and infrared analysis (bathing the artwork in infrared radiation).

In 2012, police agents searched the home of a suspect in the Isabella Stewart Gardner Museum art theft. They wore gloves and carefully bagged all evidence.

In a process known as X-ray fluorescence, objects are exposed to radiation, which makes them emit X-rays. This can reveal the composition of a sculpture or the paints and whether they are of the proper time period. X-ray fluorescence also shows up the artist's—or the forger's—fingerprints.

Forgers employ many techniques to make their new paintings look like masterpieces by long-dead artists. They bake their paintings and roll them to add the cracking, called craquelure, seen on the surface of old paintings. But careful art detectives know that cracking from old age extends randomly in all directions, while forged craquelure tends to line up in the same direction.

On a forgery painted on wood paneling, the dishonest artist may try to drill holes to look like tunnels left by worms that have eaten away at the wood over the centuries. There's just one problem with this: art detectives know that drill holes are straight, while wormholes are crooked.

Forgers also have to make sure they use the correct colors of paint if they want to escape detection. For instance, a painting created before 1800 will not include any paint of the color known as French ultramarine. It's a deep blue and was one of the first synthetic pigments or colors; it has only existed for about 200 years. The same is true for colors such as zinc white and Prussian blue.

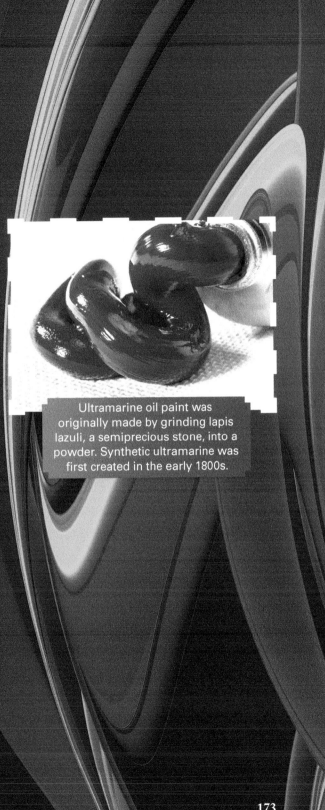

Ultramarine oil paint was originally made by grinding lapis lazuli, a semiprecious stone, into a powder. Synthetic ultramarine was first created in the early 1800s.

TIME LINE

1587   English colonists arrive at Roanoke Island, North Carolina.

1590   Governor John White returns from England to Roanoke Island; finds the colony has disappeared.

1845   Sir John Franklin and his crew set sail from Greenhithe, England, to look for the Northwest Passage aboard the HMS *Terror* and the HMS *Erebus*.

1848   The first search party is sent to look for Franklin and his crew.

1854   Inuit hunters give John Rae information about the Franklin expedition.

1857   Francis Leopold McClintock finds the only written record about the fate of Franklin and his crew.

1861   The *Amazon,* later called the *Mary Celeste*, is built in Spencer's Island, Nova Scotia.

1872   The *Mary Celeste* sets sail from New York bound for Genoa, Italy, on November 5.

        The *Mary Celeste* is found drifting aimlessly with no crew or passengers on board in December.

1885   The *Mary Celeste* runs aground off the coast of Haiti, sinks, and disappears.

1934   The American government opens a federal penitentiary on Alcatraz Island in San Francisco harbor.

1939   World War II begins.

1941   Germany invades Leningrad and takes the Amber Room from the Catherine Palace; the Siege of Leningrad begins.

1945   World War II ends.

1962   John and Clarence Anglin and Frank Morris escape from Alcatraz prison.

1984   Owen Beattie begins studying the bodies of crew from the Franklin expedition to determine how they died.

1990   Thirteen works of art are stolen from the Isabella Stewart Gardner Museum, the world's largest unsolved art heist, on March 18.

1997   Fragment from the Amber Room is recovered in Bremen, Germany.

2003   Rebuilt Amber Room opens in the Catherine Palace, Russia.

2001   Researchers claim to have found the wreck of the *Mary Celeste* off the coast of Haiti.

2012   Investigations into the Lost Colony of Roanoke discover new information hidden under patches on a 400-year-old map. It suggests the colonists may have settled at the mouth of the Chowan River, on the North Carolina coast.

2013   The FBI announces it knows who stole the works from the Isabella Stewart Gardner Museum, though no names are released and no one is arrested. The FBI also reveals it knows the artwork was transported to Philadelphia, where some of the works may have been sold.

2014   Scientists find Franklin's ship the HMS *Erebus* off Hat Island, Nunavut.

Scientists study the Alcatraz escape and determine convicts could have escaped if they had a good raft and knowledge of the tides in the area.

2015   At the mouth of the Chowan River, researchers uncover pottery that likely belonged to Roanoke colonists. Artifacts found on Hatteras Island suggest colonists from Roanoke may have settled there as well.

The FBI releases video evidence in the case of the Isabella Stewart Gardner Museum theft. The recording seems to show a rehearsal for the robbery.

PLACES TO VISIT

Lost Colony
Fort Raleigh National Historic Site, Dare County, North Carolina
Historic Jamestowne and Jamestown Settlement, Jamestown, Virginia
North Carolina Museum of History, Raleigh, North Carolina
Roanoke Island Festival Park, Manteo, Roanoke Island, North Carolina

Franklin Expedition
Canada Science and Technology Museum, Ottawa, Ontario
Glenbow Museum, Calgary, Alberta
National Maritime Museum, Greenwich, England
Royal Ontario Museum, Toronto, Ontario
Vancouver Maritime Museum, Vancouver, British Columbia

Mary Celeste
Age of Sail Heritage Museum, Port Greville, Nova Scotia
Fort Beauséjour—Fort Cumberland National Historic Site of Canada,
     Aulac, New Brunswick
Maritime Museum of the Atlantic, Halifax, Nova Scotia
Mary Celeste Memorial, Spencer's Island, Nova Scotia
Peabody Essex Museum, Salem, Massachusetts
Sippican Historical Society Museum, Marion, Massachusetts (Captain Briggs's
     hometown)

Amber Room
Catherine Palace, St. Petersburg, Russia
United States Holocaust Memorial Museum, Washington, DC

Alcatraz Prison Breakout
Alcatraz Prison Museum National Park, Alcatraz Island, San Francisco,
     California
Crime Museum, Washington, DC

Theft at the Gardner Museum
Isabella Stewart Gardner Museum, Boston, Massachusetts
Louvre Museum, Paris, France

MAIN SOURCES

Lost Colony

Don Cook. *The Long Fuse: How England Lost the American Colonies, 1760–1785.* New York: Atlantic Monthly Press, 1995.

James P. P. Horn. *A Kingdom Strange: The Brief and Tragic History of the Lost Colony of Roanoke.* New York: Basic Books, 2010.

Karen Ordahl Kupperman. *Roanoke: The Abandoned Colony.* Lanham, MD: Rowman & Littlefield Publishers, 2007.

Franklin Expedition

Owen Beattie. *Frozen in Time: The Fate of the Franklin Expedition.* Vancouver: Greystone Books, 2014.

Scott Cookman. *Ice Blink: The Tragic Fate of Sir John Franklin's Lost Polar Expedition.* New York: Wiley, 2000.

Anthony Dalton. *Sir John Franklin: Expeditions to Destiny.* Victoria, BC: Heritage, 2012.

Jeffry Blair Latta. *The Franklin Conspiracy: Cover-up, Betrayal, and the Astonishing Secret Behind the Lost Arctic Expedition.* Toronto: Hounslow Press, 2001.

David C. Woodman. *Unravelling the Franklin Mystery: Inuit Testimony.* Montreal: McGill-Queen's University Press, 1991.

Mary Celeste

Paul Begg. *Mary Celeste: The Greatest Mystery of the Sea.* New York: Longman, 2005.

Brian Hicks. *Ghost Ship: The Mysterious True Story of the Mary Celeste and Her Missing Crew.* New York: Ballantine Books, 2004.

John Gilbert Lockhart. *The Mary Celeste, and Other Strange Tales of the Sea.* London: Hart-Davis, 1952.

Valerie Martin. *The Ghost of the Mary Celeste.* New York: Nan A. Talese/Doubleday, 2014.

John Maxwell. *The 'Mary Celeste.'* London: Cape, 1979.

Amber Room

Steve Berry. *The Amber Room.* New York: Ballantine Books, 2003.

Cathy Scott-Clark. *The Amber Room: The Fate of the World's Greatest Lost Treasure.* Toronto: Viking Canada, 2004.

Alcatraz Prison Breakout

L. Campbell Bruce. *Escape from Alcatraz.* Berkeley, CA: Ten Speed Press, 2005.

Ian Crofton. *Great Escapes.* London: Quercus, 2009.

Donald MacDonald. *Alcatraz: History and Design of a Landmark.* San Francisco: Chronicle Books, 2012.

John A. Martini. *Fortress Alcatraz: Guardian of the Golden Gate.* Berkeley, CA: Ten Speed Press, 2004.

Theft at the Gardner Museum

Ulrich Boser. *The Gardner Heist: A True Story of the World's Largest Unsolved Art Theft.* New York: Smithsonian Books/HarperCollins, 2009.

Martin Caparrós. *Valfierno: The Man Who Stole the Mona Lisa.* New York: Atria Books, 2008.

Dorothy Hoobler. *The Crimes of Paris: A True Story of Murder, Theft, and Detection.* New York: Little, Brown, 2009.

Thomas McShane. *The Stolen Masterpiece Tracker: Memoirs of the FBI's #1 Art Sleuth.* Fort Lee, NJ: Barricade Books, 2006.

Robert Noah. *The Man Who Stole the Mona Lisa.* New York: St. Martin's Press, 1998.

R. A. Scotti. *Vanished Smile: The Mysterious Theft of Mona Lisa.* New York: Knopf Books, 2009.

FURTHER READING

Lost Colony
Judith Herbst. *Lands of Mystery*. Minneapolis: Lerner Publications, 2005.

Anne Rooney. *Strange Places*. Mankato, MN: Smart Apple Media, 2010.

Alex Simmons. *Mysteries of the Past*. New York: Children's Press, 2005.

Nancy Ward. *Sir Walter Raleigh: Founding the Virginia Colony*. New York: Crabtree Publishing, 2006.

Franklin Expedition
Owen Beattie. *Buried in Ice*. Mississauga, ON: Random House of Canada, 1992.

Rose Blue and Corinne J. Naden. *Exploring the Arctic*. Chicago: Raintree, 2004.

Mary Celeste
Sharon Dalgleish. *It's a Mystery*. Philadelphia, PA: Chelsea House, 2005.

Alex Simmons. *Mysteries of the Past*. New York: Children's Press, 2005.

Rachel Wright. *The True Mystery of the Mary Celeste*. New York: Scholastic, 2001.

Jane Yolen and Heidi E. Y. Stemple. *The Mary Celeste: An Unsolved Mystery from History*. New York: Simon & Schuster Books for Young Readers, 1999.

Amber Room
Elizabeth MacLeod. *The Kids Book of Canada at War*. Toronto: Kids Can Press, 2007.

Elizabeth MacLeod. *Royal Murder*. Toronto: Annick Press, 2008.

Alcatraz Prison Breakout
Paul Dowswell. *True Stories of Escape*. London, UK: Usborne Publishing, 2007.

Lori Haskins Houran. *Breakout! Escape from Alcatraz*. New York: Random House, 1996.

Marilyn Tower Oliver. *Alcatraz Prison*. Berkeley Heights, NJ: Enslow Publishers, 1998.

Susan Sloate. *Mysteries Unwrapped: The Secrets of Alcatraz*. New York: Sterling, 2008.

Stephanie Watson. *The Escape from Alcatraz*. Edina, MN: ABDO, 2012.

Theft at the Gardner Museum
Pat Hutchins. *The Mona Lisa Mystery*. New York: Greenwillow Books, 1981.

Rick Jacobson. *The Mona Lisa Caper*. Toronto: Tundra Books, 2005.

J. Patrick Lewis. *The Stolen Smile*. Mankato, MN.: Creative Editions, 2004.

IMAGE CREDITS

ACKNOWLEDGMENTS

It was great to work again with one of my favorite teams of wonderfully creative people. Chandra Wohleber is a terrific editor and helped me so much with this manuscript. I always appreciate the fantastic skill of designer Sheryl Shapiro, who made this book, and so many others, look so great. I also want to thank photo researcher Sandra Booth for her incredible persistence and skill in uncovering an amazing variety of wonderful photos.

Many thanks as well to managing editor Rivka Cranley, copy editor Catherine Dorton, and proofreader Judy Phillips. Thanks for all you did to improve this book. I also appreciate the assistance and support of everyone at Annick Press, especially Brigitte Waisberg, marketing manager.

As well, I'd like to thank Kate Kluge for help with German translations, and Dr. Douglas MacLeod, Chair, Royal Architectural Institute of Canada Centre for Architecture, Athabasca University. I also always appreciate the help of the librarians of the Toronto Public Library system, especially those at the Leaside Library.

Thanks as ever to Dad, John, and Douglas. And special thanks and love to Paul, who makes so many difficulties simply dissolve and vanish!

INDEX